GENESEE AND SCOTT

By
Pete Herbig

**The true story of a boy's sexual abuse, and
the man's long journey to recovery**

If I get it all down on paper, it's no longer
Inside of me, threatening the life it belongs to
And I feel like I'm naked in front of the crowd
'Cause these words are my diary, screaming out loud
And I know that you'll use them, however you want to.[1]

Prologue

Upstage center is lit with dull red and blue lights, backlighting the instruments, amplifiers, and other equipment onstage—just barely. A man scurries across the stage, checking equipment and making adjustments where necessary. Wolf whistles and howls pierce the warm, muggy night, a thin cloud of smoke wavering right above the crowd's head. The Bicycle Day riders—high on LSD, with smiles on their faces and large, round eyes—begin to kick the ground as energy surges through their veins. Laughter and anticipation fill the air. Everyone knows what is going to happen, yet they have no clue how it will start, or how it will end. Cigarettes are lit, and joints passed. The crowd lets out a collective howl.

A beach ball is tossed in the air, then another, the crowd cheering and laughing with each punch. T-shirts, cutoffs, summer dresses, tie-dye shirts—the summer is here and church is about to start. Another collective cheer sets the whole crowd on fire. The gentlemen are late—not by much, not by musician standards. The pre-show rituals are performed as the stage manager waits, not patiently, with flashlight in hand. Slowly, the crew make their way, off stage left to the bottom of the stairs. discussing the night's menu and setup. After a group hug and a moment of silence, the stage manager gets on the radio: "House lights to half, house to quarter, out." Simultaneously, the stage lights are turned off and the pre-show music fades. The crowd erupts into an electric roar. Another round of joints are quickly lit and passed. The stage manager turns on his flashlight and dashes up the stage-left stairs, then quickly turns to shine his light on the stairs as the band members make their way up to the stage, then spotlights the wires and cables in their path.

Each member makes his way to his place onstage, and the techs peel off to their own stations. A gentleman—dressed in black T-shirt and jeans, with long, curly Jim Morrison-esque dark hair—makes his way from stage left to stage right. He glances at the crowd, half joker, half madman, and takes a seat in front of a row of pedals, picks up his guitar. A quick bass drum beat from the drummer sets the crowd off again. They're ready for fun—or for a fight. The man in his chair checks the dials of his guitar, occasionally glancing out at the crowd with a wide grin.

The bass player and guitarists pull up their axes and strap them on. The man in black makes a few last adjustments and settles back. The conga player gives a few taps with fingers and thumbs, listening to the tuning, then quickly reaches down and grabs his key, makes one last adjustment to the head. The guitars start with an easy strum, giving the feet permission to move. The crowd starts a slow and deliberate undulation, to the measured melodic beats. The song picks up with the addition of a drumbeat. Then the congas come to life and the crowd blasts a long bellow of approval.

"I opened up my eyes to see a land of sunny rocks and funny trees,"[2] the song starts with a harmony of voices and the crowd explodes. They know the song, they want the song, and they need it. The song meanders on, each line bringing more loud agreement from the sold-out crowd, swaying, yelping, smiling, and cheering. They approve of the band's choice for an opener.

The man in black with the mop of curly hair plucks his guitar while shaking the neck, providing audio depth to the song. He is waiting like a big cat to pounce, stalking each instrument he hears, glancing over to feel their next move. This song was built for Michael Houser. He watches his bandmates intently, waiting to add his one- or two-string strums. He, like the wolves in the crowd, is waiting for the kill. And kill he will, again and again.

As the lyrics end and the music carries on, there is a quick and sudden riff on the ride-tom and the song takes off. Michael comes in with a wail of his guitar. His right foot furiously works his effects pedal, his fingers running all over the strings, chasing each other like the last witches from Salem. He looks across the stage to John Bell—lead singer, songwriter, friend—with a shit-eating grin.

Michael met John when they both attended the University of Georgia. A North Carolina boy, Michael fit in with his new friend and soon to be bandmate. They gathered members along the way and called themselves Widespread Panic, after the panic attacks that Michael suffered as a child.

The band would go on to become one of the best first-generation jam bands on the circuit and is still one of my favorites. Widespread Panic would travel in the footprint of the Grateful Dead and the Allman Brothers Band—tour, tour, and then tour some more.

Jam bands make their name, and their living, off of live performances, not studio albums. The road can be grueling, and when you're playing two hundred, two hundred fifty nights a year, it becomes extremely hard on bands, crews, and families. But the Panic were ready and they went head-first into the early 1990s, when the scene really took off. They would still be one of the top bands standing and producing in the genre decades later. As this scene is very cutthroat, that's saying something.

I first saw Widespread Panic on the 1992 H.O.R.D.E tour, which included Blues Traveler, Phish, Aquarium Rescue Unit, and Spin Doctors. Panic were peaking and they sounded great. They didn't know it at the time, but Michael Houser was on a collision course with a thief who would steal everything he had.

Everyone is dealt a hand of cards. Some people get the poverty card, some the money card; some the tall card, some the short card. Some get the smart card, others not so much. As we get older, we create some cards on our own—graduate from high school, college, professional training. Some are forced into our hands by others—Mom makes you take piano lessons; you get the music card. All these unique little attributes that makes us up and give us definition as a person.

In July 2002, Michael Houser would leave the summer tour due to his health. On August 10, 2002, Michael Houser passed away and left this earth, leaving a wife, a child, friends, family, his band, and his fans behind.

What do you do when you get a bad card inserted into your hand—something you do not want, did not create, that could kill you? There's no way to exchange it for another—you just have to play the cards you are dealt. And hope you are alive at the end.

CHAPTER 1

I got in the game in 1971, in a place called Newington, Connecticut. I came home to a three-family row house, across from a hill that descended into a huge bowl containing a couple of baseball fields and a lot of open space. We had a small, shared backyard, and behind it a grass patch, a wooded area. The wooded area was a little swampy, worse after a rain.

I am the youngest of my family, with one brother older by four years, my other brother Bruce, older by six, and my sister, older by seven. You can see by the age differential that I was not exactly planned for. My dad wasn't around all that much. He traveled quite a bit, working for a medical company based in Switzerland.

I remember our house pretty well. In through the front door, stairs going up on the left. Straight ahead was a wide opening with a small kitchen on the right and dining room across from the kitchen. To the left, across from the kitchen entrance, was the door to the basement. A sliding-glass door led down into the shared driveway and backyard. My dad and I used to sit there and feed the squirrels. I was unable to pronounce "squirrels," so I called them "keels."

To the right of the front door was the living room, with a couch and TV. When my dad was home and took naps, I would sit my little butt in the crook of his knees on the couch. I would sit and listen to the Boston Pops on PBS and watch a gentleman named Arthur Fiedler conduct the show. I enjoyed watching his sharp, quick motions. Plus, the music was nice.

One day when we kids got cabin fever, we got snow-geared-up

and went out in the yard. There was just a dusting of snow, but it was still cold outside. We brought out our trusty dog, Rip (my father named our German shepherd Euripides), on a leash that my sister held. My sister, my brother Bruce, and my other brother made their way over to the woods, which had pockets of ice with potential for ice skating. My sister and Bruce went out with Rip and glided across the ice a little. My other brother was soon to follow, but not too far behind.

The floor of the woods looked like some kind of horror film. Dead branches, tree roots, and large and small rocks were all frozen in the couple inches of water that sat on the ground. Old, dried leaves that never made it to the floor in the fall still flew every time the wind blew, giving you a false sense of time. Some large sheets of ice had frozen over the last couple of days; some stood by themselves, interrupted by the root systems, or rocks. And then, we saw a large sheet of ice standing on its own, interrupted only by trees and stumps and roots—plenty of room for some boot skating.

As I was standing on the edge, my sister gestured me over and gave me Rip's leash. I was never allowed to hold his leash, so I thought I must be a big kid now. But nope, just an idiot, because as my sister and Bruce skated away, taking bigger strides without the hindrance of the dog, Rip spotted something in the distance and took off.

In one second, I went from upright and vertical to being pulled, horizontally, across this root-infested ice by a seventy-five-pound German shepherd. Luckily, the big coat and snow pants took the brunt of the bruising, but I was being pulled hard and jostled a lot. My hand was looped in the leash, so letting go wasn't really an option. My head missed a skunk cabbage by inches; trees seemed to speed by, upside-down and backward.

I could hear my siblings call out for Rip to stop, but that was not happening. I was too scared to make any noises and at three years old I did not know the words "shit" or "fuck" yet, so I could not find any verbiage to meet the moment.

Rip's running was intermittent, due to his traction. When

he hit the ice, his paws slipped—his nails couldn't grip it. But when he made it to some dead leaves, or a root sticking out of the ice, he gripped and ripped and I would speed up again.

Luckily, eventually Rip went left and I went right. I got the leash off my hand and he went back to my mom, who was back outside by this time ("Can't even leave them alone for a second!"). My sister and Bruce came over, giggling, and helped me up. Feigning concern, they brought me to my mother. I appeared alright because I was not crying—I think in the thrill of it all, I didn't think to cry. I was just glad I didn't pee or poop myself.

Around this time, my dad's dad passed away. My father moved us back to his home town of Syracuse, New York, to take care of his widowed mother.

The house filled with boxes, which my dad helped pack before he left. He wasn't there the day we moved—it was up to my mother to manage everything. After the movers packed everything up, she packed us four kids, ranging from three (me) to ten (sister), plus a large dog

and two cats, into our red VW bus. It was three weeks before my fourth birthday. One of the cats roamed around the bus as we drove and about half an hour into the ride it pooped under the gas pedal. We now could not go over 45 miles an hour all the way there. There were two feet of snow on the ground when we reached Syracuse.

As the youngest, I surely did not receive a vote in the matter of moving, nor did any of my siblings. My sister was pissed to be leaving the number-one public school education system in the country, and her two saxophone teachers. This would be her fourth move by the age ten.

The three of them ended up enrolled in the local Catholic school, Our Lady of Solace. My sister was really bummed by the total downgrade in academics and would soon take things into her own hands when it came to her education.

We moved into a house on Ramsey Avenue—brick bottom,

white top—at the top of a hill. It was a ten-minute walk to my grandmother's house. I would find out several years later that famous architect Ward Wellington Ward designed much of the neighborhood and previously lived right around the corner. All of my schools were within a fifteen-minute walk: Our Lady of Solace, Aaron T. Levy Middle School, and William Nottingham High School (go Bulldogs!).

On our left, our neighbors had a daughter my brother Bruce's age, and she had a younger brother a couple of years older than me. On our right was a truck driver who used to park his rig in the driveway, which I thought was cool. A few years later, a new couple moved in, who would have three kids and a crapload of puppies. Across the street was a family with two kids younger than me, and their neighbor had a couple of younger kids also.

There were kids everywhere in my neighborhood, ranging from ten years older to ten years younger than me. We could have fielded two full baseball teams, and in fact, we did. We used a driveway as home base, the medians as first and third base, and the manhole cover as second.

Down the hill from our house was Meadowbrook, a stream that ran the entire course of the street. Nearby Barry Park held one of the local basketball courts and attracted top talent from all over the city. With a jungle gym, tennis courts, and a couple of baseball diamonds, it was hopping on summer nights. The park would be full of moms and kids, the tennis courts would be full and adult softball (drinking) teams usually had at least two games rolling. Plus, division one, two, and three basketball teams played until the sun went down, which was fierce and fun to watch. Across the street was a large pond that you could jog or bike around.

Nearby Nottingham Plaza held the local pharmacy, liquor store, hardware store, and gas station. Then there was Johnny's Pizza, the best pizza in the land. Peter's Plaza had Peter's IGA, a local grocery chain, and other shops.

If you left my house and went left, that brought you to East Genesee Street. Going left out of the intersection, you would go down three blocks until you crossed over Scott Ave.

My great grandfather Charles "Carl" Herbig was born in Germany in 1844 and died in 1896 in Syracuse, New York. He had a son named Frank Joseph, born in Germany in 1877. According to census documents, the Herbig clan arrived in the Syracuse area around 1894. My other great grandfather also died in Syracuse, in 1957.

In 1899 in Syracuse, New York, my grandfather Francis John Herbig was born. He grew up on the east side of town, when the Erie Canal still ran through the center of the city, and so did the railways. He was trained to be an industrial fabric cleaner. He cleaned large-scale curtains and linens. Most of the older family members were tailors by trade.

My grandfather on my dad's side was born, grew up, and passed away in Syracuse. My family didn't talk much about my dad's older relatives. The ones from Germany knew Germans weren't liked all that much in the United States so, they said nothing about the old country. The younger relatives didn't speak German so, they were ignored by the older German speaking relatives.. They tried so hard to assimilate to the American culture that they never spoke of their own.

My maternal grandmother grew up in Ithaca. She and her brother Eddie would walk across town daily and deliver newspapers. Farmers still met to graze their animals and share the news of the day. My grandmother is also famous for contracting, and surviving, the international Spanish flu of 1918, which killed anywhere between 40 and 100 million people.

My grandmother grew up Catholic, like most good Irish people at the time. She went to private school and went through all the religious ceremonies. She came to Syracuse after high school for college and started her nursing degree soon after.

My grandparents met when my grandfather's mother was

dying. Apparently, he was in and out of the hospital quite a bit, and I guess this quality endeared him to my grandmother. She started to talk to my grandfather in the elevator and after a few conversations they decided to go out on a date. And that, as they say, is that. So, there's that creepy aspect of my family.

They married and moved to the east side of town, where they would have two sons: my uncle, who is older by four years, and my dad. My grandfather does not get any rave reviews on parenting. My sister affectionately refers to him as the Kraut. All four would reside in the house until the kids went to college, and my grandfather passed away in 1973. My grandmother stayed in the house—*she* is nothing short of a narcissist. If it does not involve her or something she cares about, she couldn't care less. You and I are merely pieces in her world and if you do not bend her way, you're an idiot.

When I was four years old, my mom stayed home and took care of me and my siblings after they returned from school. I would make my first friend at church, where my family met Garrett's family and we were forever linked. For the next nine years I would see Garrett at least five days a week, including in summer. My mom would take care all of us—Garrett, his sister, and all four of us—during the summer months.

It was a good thing I met Garrett because my siblings and I are quite different. My brothers had no athletic inclinations; my sister was drawn to the worlds of art, stage, and entertainment. All of my siblings read quite a bit. My parents both had taught school, and do not suffer ignorance lightly.

An English major who read a lot and liked to garden, my mom was a buffer for my dad; she talked more and was more empathetic. She was a Jersey girl, the youngest of four whose childhood was spent with her dad away in Europe on the World War II gig. But my mom was never really questioned me about who I was or how I felt. Neither of my parents did.

Garrett gave me an outlet to run around and go crazy,

which we both needed at that age. He came over every school morning and stayed at my house with me and my mom. His sister, along with my brothers and sister, would then all go to Our Lady of Solace. After school, everyone came back to our place until one of Garrett's parents came and picked them up.

Those days were fun. If you went to the bottom of my street, Meadowbrook ran down the center of the road. There were dump trucks, scooper trucks, worker men, and all the tools, placing these huge flat rocks at angles and creating new banks for the stream. All the four-year-olds were happy, and all the moms were happy. My mom would bring us down and we would watch for hours, sitting in the grass under some trees, the men waving at us.

After our truck-watching, we headed home for lunch, then nap, and then we would go outside and play in the yard under the watchful eye of Rip. No one would step foot in our yard if the dog was outside. I turned five that spring—in the fall, Garrett and I would be off to kindergarten.

That summer, another person was added to my life: Dan. Dan lived a lot closer than Garrett—I could see Dan's house from my backyard. He also had four kids in his family: an older brother by four years, who kindly saved me from drowning at the local JCC one day; and two sisters, one two years older, and one two years younger. Dan is exactly two weeks older than I am. We spent the summer around my house, just tearing up whatever we could find as best we could.

That fall, Garrett, Dan, and I started kindergarten at Our Lady of Perpetually Shitty (formally known as Our Lady of Solace), a K-8 Catholic school a half-mile from home. The church was right across the street, with the rectory next to that and the convent on the backside of the school. It had a gym, library, lunchroom, and band room. We started off with half-days and then went home to my mom, to screw off until the other kids got home.

Our Lady of Solace was a brick, two-story building shaped like an L, set on a hill. When I started at Solace, there were still nuns that would grab you if you didn't listen or displeased them. This nun in seventh grade tried to grab the short hairs on the back of one of my siblings' neck, and all three siblings threw their hand over to knock her arm off. She got the idea not to try that with anyone in my family.

My grandfather, my dad's dad, was born left-handed and a Catholic. Since the left-handed were considered an abomination in the eyes of the lord, they would tie my grandpa's arm to his side, or to his desk, to "nurture" the use of his right hand. If they didn't feel like tying him down, they would just crack the back of his left hand with a wooden ruler or yardstick every time they caught him using it in class. Catholic educators sure do love their violence.

Me and my brother eating watermelon at some parade picnic. I was about 5 years old here. The belt I am wearing was probably as long as I was high.

We fell into a routine, which would stay the same for the year. But things started to change with my eldest brother, Bruce Jr. From that time on, nothing in the family would ever be the same. He started fucking off in school, skipping class, and coming home late. He was extremely disrespectful to everyone in the family. This was not your average teenage rebellion, or displeasure of the move to Syracuse. There was real anger behind his actions.

Bruce was the Irish twin to my sister, meaning that my sister and Bruce were born in the same 365 days. He was not into sports, was a little chubby, and didn't really get into after-school activities, though like most Catholic boys he ended up being an altar boy. He had trouble making friends, but then he'd moved three times by the time we settled in Syracuse. Trust is hard to build if you're afraid to make friends because you may be uprooted at any second. Trusting my parents might stay in Syracuse must have been hard for him. At that time, all I knew was that the older kids were yelling about things I didn't understand.

Even though there was growing static between Bruce Jr. and my parents, we just carried on as families do, I guess. I started first grade and began a full day of school, walking home with my siblings, then chaos, then maybe a snack. Being born the bottom of four children sucks. I had no voice, no vote, last pickings at dinner, and shit always rolled downhill. I would just run out of oxygen, because it was all being swallowed by my siblings, just trying to get by in their day. Plus, the issues between Bruce Jr. and my parents took more and more of their time for me away.

CHAPTER 2

A round this time, my sister began hanging out at a local community theater, The Salt City Center for the Performing Arts. It was in an old Adath Yeshurun temple that was built in 1921 and vacated in 1971. In 1973, a gentleman named Joe Lotito, who was running a makeshift theater in a downtown warehouse, proposed that his theater move into the temple. So in 1974 the temple became an independent, community-responsive, run-by-the-seat-of-your-pants playhouse.

The 65,000 square feet included two theaters. It had a Greek/Roman facade, with four huge pillars in front of the red doors; the doors had stained-glass windows, with some of the broken panes replaced with Plexiglas. On each side of the doors was a black iron light fixture, adding a certain mystique, and to the left was a white sign, lit up at night: a picture of Shakespeare in tights, with his left arm around the top of a salt shaker. In big black letters it read salt city center for the performing arts. But since the original name was the Salt City Playhouse, it would be called that by me, my sister, and most others associated with it.

Upon entering into the lobby, you would notice the cold, dark cement floor. To the left was the box office booth, with a sliding-glass window, a notebook with a pen attached by a string. In the booth was Ruth Cope, whose job it was to make sure everyone signed in and out. She wore all-black heavy dresses and sensible shoes—a Quaker, she dressed the part.

To the right were two deep-brown wooden doors—usually propped open, unless there was a show on—that led to the main stage. The long pews were also deep-brown, from old wood with wide rings. The cushions were purple, dulled by age, dust, and wear. The end of each pew had a bas-relief Star of David inscribed on it. Huge, vaulted ceilings—probably about forty or fifty feet from ceiling to floor—housed four giant chandeliers that lit the theater. The stage was built of wood and about three feet high. Behind it, downstairs, was the scenic shop; upstairs led to classrooms, props, and dressing rooms. When you looked from the stage to the back of the theater, you could get a full view of the balcony, with its orange velvet–colored seats, and the lighting booth for the main stage.

Back in the lobby, the wide gray institutional stairs took you up to the second and third floors, where the "new addition" had been added onto the back of the temple: a yellow building attached long after the original building went up, which held a kindergarten, preschool, and kitchen. The upstairs on the second and third floors, along with the new addition, held several classrooms, a dance studio, lounge, and dressing rooms.

Back on the main floor, on the other side of the stairs, a hallway led to the second theater. It was the old cafeteria and had four support beams in the room, which could not be removed due to structural issues. On three sides of the four pillars, theater seats were built—but with no rise to be able to see the stage better. The stage was surrounded by seats on three sides. The fourth side had a black wall providing a backstage. Seating capacity for the small theater was a hundred and forty.

My sister hung out here constantly, acting in plays and doing stage work: wardrobe, climb and fix lights. It was a real community theater, where you had to pitch in to make a show work. She did a little bit of everything, got to watch a lot of things and determine what she liked; it was also around this time that she began to write. She sucked me and my brother into it too, which got us out of the house.

My brother and I ended up being in a production called *Not Even a Mouse,* a play based around a Christmas mouse, where the crowd sang along with Christmas carols. I didn't know it at the time, but that was how my sister kept my brother and me out of Bruce Jr's path of destruction. But only until the Christmas season was over.

Unfortunately, my parents did not have the money for tee-ball, so I couldn't play with Dan and Garrett in the spring. I was stuck around the house more, and my mom started to go back to teaching, so things were different at home. My sister was in charge and the playhouse was an escape for the three of us.

Bruce Jr. was being a dick to everyone. At the time, he was just generally short with me, and I learned from his curt responses not to interact with him. He was a huge jerk to everyone else: vicious and aggressive with my sister and brother. I was always on pins and needles, full of anxiety, which I could not understand or explain. I didn't tell anyone and just tried not to cause any problems.

The blowups with my parents were always upsetting to me. I hid in my bedroom as much as I could, reading Disney books we had for kids, Greek tragedies, and other short stories; or listening to the radio. The music that was on the radio then is called classic rock now—but back then it was not yet classic. That year Fleetwood Mac released *Rumours,* Sex Pistols *Never Mind the Bollocks, Here's the Sex Pistols,* The Clash *The Clash,* Eric Clapton *Slowhand,* Ramones *Rocket to Russia,* David Bowie *Heroes,* and Steely Dan *Aja,* to name just a few. It was prime time for the first generation of blues interpretation from Europe and America.

It was a great comfort to me to have that music. Music has always been a comfort, a place I go when things are not good, then and now.

That summer we took a family vacation to Maine and went camping. We saw Thunder Hole and I ended up slipping off a rock and fell in the drink by our campsite. My dad had to race downstream and pull me out. I remember sitting by the campfire, cold as shit because it had been raining the whole week. One more day of rain and we packed and headed for a hotel. Then, that night, in a dark theater in early August 1977, I saw *Star Wars.* That was my first real exposure to science fiction on a screen, and it was great.

Second grade started at the end of August and I was back full-time with Garrett and Dan. Except for a few people who came and went, I would be with the same twenty or so kids from kindergarten to sixth grade. School was the same routine, but my sister no longer went to Solace; she went to a local Catholic high school, which she actually hated more. My brother and I would walk to school or get a ride with Garrett's dad. Bruce Jr. would walk by himself, on purpose.

Things between Bruce Jr. and the rest of our family were profoundly strained. He was getting into trouble more and more, generally just not giving a fuck. It put me on edge, making being around him very hard, and at times scary. Fear of being home was a very real thing for me and I hated that I could find no comfort there. Bruce would act out in school or outside of school and just brought chaos to the house. My parents were constantly focused on his fuck-ups.

Just before Christmas, my sister wanted to know if I wanted to audition for a musical, *Pippin.* I auditioned and got a part, which was exciting because I would have actual lines to speak. But I would need to go to rehearsal after school and on weekends, plus do shows on weekday and weekend nights. I would play the part of Theo, Pippin's friend. I had about fifteen lines and a pet duck.

Production started after the New Year, 1979. My sister and I rehearsed my lines. She would come home and grab me, and we would take the bus going downtown to Genesee Street, at the bottom of the hill the theater sat on. Some members of the cast would already be there, and others would roll in. A few people came from class, but most members came from their day job.

We kept our street clothes and winter jackets on inside. In Syracuse at the end of January, the temperature is known to hover in the teens to low twenties during the day, and the theater was almost as cold—heating the whole place was not an option as the main theater was cavernous. We stood in front of the clanging heaters, winter jackets over our costumes, trying to grab whatever heat we could on those frigid nights, as the heaters banged and clanged like a sound stage for *Willy Wonka*. When someone's scene was called you could hear them curse under their breath. The part of Theo only makes an appearance in the second act, so I would sit and watch the entire first act.

My mother made my costume and it was very similar to Pippin's: green polyester pants with brown patterned leggings that went up to my knees. My mother knitted the top, which was shaped like a tank top, but wider in the shoulders; it was dyed a dark, muddy gray, like institutional oatmeal. With the lights off in the theater I must have looked like a little night-light with my very white skin.

At the end of February, my cousin C came to live with us. She was older than my sister, which my sister appreciated because she was becoming dead tired of her brothers. C is one of the daughters of my mom's oldest sister. I really liked having her around —she stepped in where my siblings could not and played catch with me. She was magical because she could catch the ball with one hand and smoke a cigarette with another. Choke on that, Superman! She would also drive me to rehearsal in her green Volkswagen bus, which had to be pushed down the street sometimes to pop the clutch, because it had a bad starter.

The show was set to open the weekend of February 16 and run until the weekend of March 9. We had rehearsed a lot and pulled a couple late nights; I remember just curling up and lying on a pew. I was still eight years old and the rest of the cast and crew were mostly college students and young adults.

I was truly excited for the first show, and terrified, but too young to realize the enormity of what was about to happen. Once I got the first few lines out I felt much better and grinned to myself. I did not want to fuck anything up.

So, I hit all my lines, and no one ran over me as we moved across the stage. Success! We lined up for our final bow, and I was one of the last people out. My mother in the show looked at me and extended her arm, as if to present me to the audience. I walked out a few steps past her and took the first bow of my life, in front of an audience of probably about three hundred people, maybe more. I walked back and took her hand; we did our group bows, then house to black.

To this day, that has been one of the most powerful moments in my life. I have never been able to duplicate that sensation again. There I was, almost eight years old and in front of this explosion of clapping and cheering—and it was magical. Nothing in my life has compared to that feeling, except the birth of my children. Not even the Philadelphia Eagles winning the Super Bowl. I think I was up until about one a.m. on opening night, unable to sleep from all the excitement. It built some good feelings in me and what I was doing—a leap in self-esteem, which was difficult to acquire in my house.

The morning after the Saturday show, my sister came into the living room, while I was on the couch watching cartoons, and pushed a newspaper into my hand. In big, bold words were written: *pippin* is kingly. The article named every cast member, and I came across my name, completely in awe. I had to read the sentence twice: "She's the young widow, with a young son (Peter Herbig) whose winning ways keep Pippin around—but just for a little while."

I had never seen my name in the paper before, and I'd never really thought about how the media would cover the musical, but I was glad they got my name right. I finished up the last show of the first weekend walking on air and brought the paper to school that Monday.

We still had three weekends to go, but it felt a lot easier now. My parents and grandmother came the second weekend and Garrett and Dan's parents came on the third weekend. A bunch of my family's friends came too, and it was nice to have community support.

Friday, March 9, was the first of the last three shows. When I arrived at the theater I went upstairs and got into costume, to practice blocking. As I walked to the door, the other actors walked in front of me to open it, and I followed them down the hall. As they went around the corner, they split apart and I looked up: there in front of the dressing room doors, lined all around the exterior of the hallway, was the entire cast.

My first thought was *I am in trouble.* Truth and justice had come for me.

Everyone was looking at me and grinning, bubbling with anticipation. Not only was the cast there, so were the stagehands, the lighting techs, and the audio team. They all started in, singing me "Happy Birthday." A huge cake with candles emerged from the men's dressing room, held out by our costume director, in a fabulous sequin halter top, jeans, and heels, trying his best not to blow the candles out.

I was presented with the first piece. I took it and thanked everyone. As I ate it, I was very, very grateful.

At this time, Bruce's behavior overshadowed holidays, birthdays, any downtime that might otherwise be mined for fun or peace. He was stealing money for booze and drugs, plus he would not adhere to my parents' curfew. All this static he created made it very hard to concentrate on my own life. Everything was a knockdown, drag-out fight between Bruce and my parents.

A family culture changes when such a disruptive force is placed within it. The parents focus resources on the disruption, attempting to quell it. The siblings deal with the disruption however they can. In my case, having to deal with fear and anger drained my energy for other facets of my life. I hid in my room as much as I could, trying to find a safe haven. One night during this time, a crying teenager and his parent appeared at our front door, flipping out on my dad about how Bruce had assaulted their son, for no other reason than being alive. Having seen what Bruce could do outside the house made being home that much more unsettling.

The last show went off without a hitch, and I headed upstairs to where the costume director was putting on makeup. I had heard of *The Rocky Horror Picture Show* at the Westcott Theater— I hadn't had a chance to see it, as the midnight showing was past my bedtime. But I knew my sister and Bruce had snuck out to see it, and I had heard all about it and knew the songs, since the record spun constantly in the house.

It was fun watching the cast get ready, and everyone looked great. I said goodbye to them and thanked them for the cake. I hugged every female in the show, and they again wished me Happy Birthday.

I was unsure what to do next. I went and changed out of my costume. Members of the ensemble were already talking about parts for *Jesus Christ Superstar,* which was next on the theater agenda. I said my goodbyes, and everyone said "see you around," except I was just going back to second grade.

After the musical, I came back to what I had been missing at home; Bruce's fighting, drinking, and drugging. He wasn't even going to school, much less handing in homework. As his behavior got more reckless and scary, my anxiety at home was exacerbated. Grounding him only made him stick around the house, being a dick.

As I was around the house more now, I experienced his attitude firsthand. He was dismissive to all of us and getting complaints from school for not doing homework, talking back, and being disruptive. He was stealing my sister's babysitting money and rifling through my mom's purse and anything else that wasn't nailed down, and using drugs and alcohol on almost a daily basis.

I hated being home. I hated the atmosphere and the fear and anxiety it created inside of me. Bruce was nothing if not antisocial. Anything that happened in the house, you could be sure he would have a negative take on it.

Tax Day, to most, is a harrowing experience, but if you were be-tween the ages of seven and fourteen and you lived in my area, it meant the beginning of Salt Springs baseball. Dan's dad ran the local fast-pitch tee-ball league on our side of town. This year, my parents got the money together for me to play. I was on the gold team, along with Garrett and Dan. I wasn't much of a hitter, but I could field some. I mostly just enjoyed being with my friends and was glad to be out of the house again. The drama at home made everyday things so much harder.

We practiced a few times and then started games for the season at Lemoyne College. Each team was called by the name of their shirt color: Red, Navy, Green... I would ride my bike up the hill and look down on all these kids in their colored shirts, off to their games, like giant crayons walking down the street.

It was hard to lead a normal life when chaos always awaited my return home. It's hard to really do anything when you have to contest with such a dynamic environment in a place that's supposed to be comforting, where you're supposed to be able to get away from your problems. You can't focus on what's in front of you if you're wondering if you're going to be safe when you return home.

Bruce brought fear and anxiety to my house daily. Chaos. Fighting and threatening me and my siblings, yelling at and dis-obeying my parents. Whether it was being stoned, assaulting someone, stealing money—it all lead to the chaos one way or an-other, day after day. Bruce was a violent criminal who had yet to be arrested.

We went to Massachusetts, to my mom's parents' house, for a week every summer. This year, we went to my grandfather's Knights of Columbus picnic at their church—a fairly big event, with several generations of people attending. My father used to be a Knight, so he knew the secret handshake and whatnot. It was a fun event, with games for the kids, beer for the adults, and lobsters and clams cooking everywhere.

About two and half hours and six sodas in, I was wandering around when I heard the second worst scream of my life. The sound was like nothing I had ever heard in my life—loud and very frightening. It sounded like fear. Everyone looked around and people moved in the direction of the sound. I saw some commotion and heard someone yell "Get some help!" A semi-circle formed around one of the tables, in front of the boiling lobster pots.

I made my way around to the back to see what was going on. On the ground an older man—beet-red, sweating profusely, with a towel in his mouth—was screaming in pain. One of the lobster pots had tipped over and fallen on his leg. His ankle skin was bubbling and red and I could see the inside ball of his ankle. Vacations were supposed to be places of refuge, quiet, and rejuvenation. It felt chaos was following me wherever I went, even though I was not the victim of this dreadful event.

That summer, I enjoyed pissing my other brother off to no end. Now *that* was fun. Bruce and my other brother rarely, if ever, did anything together. The one thing they had done together was play Dungeons & Dragons, but that had come to an end. My brother had a friend over one day, they were playing D&D, and I wanted in.

After I'd pestered them for a while, my brother threw the basic blue D&D book at me and said, "If you can read it and make a character, you can play." His friend gave a grunted "ha" under his breath as I walked away, and they continued.

Fuck that! Eight-year-old me accepted his challenge.

I went to the dining room table and started to read the book. I had to go and ask my mom for help with some words, but about an hour and a half later, I went back to my brother. I handed him the book and gave him my character sheet: a dwarf fighter. He was pissed but looked it over and found it satisfactory. In a huff, he let me join the game.

I only had four hit points, so I was dead within an hour. I went and cried to my mom, distraught. But that day opened the door for my older brother and me to do something together—to this day one of the only things that we've ever done together—and it allowed him to play without having to rely on Bruce or his friends. Plus, we were already in the same bedroom.

Bruce's erratic behavior overshadowed everything. A mistrust started between my sister, my parents, my cousin C, and Bruce. Bruce was getting into trouble, but he couldn't figure out where my parents were getting their information. My cousin was six years older than Bruce, so she was a lot wiser than my parents when it came to the younger generation and what kind of trouble teenage kids get into. My cousin worked during the day and went out sometimes at night, but she was mostly home witnessing the carnage. I know she was the one telling my parents what Bruce was up to. I often saw one of my parents, along with C, whispering in the kitchen, or the downstairs hallway.

CHAPTER 3

In 1979, I started third grade. I had one of the crabbier nuns for third grade, which took the air out of learning. Bruce was in ninth grade now, my sister in tenth, and my other brother in seventh. Bruce and my sister now went to the local high school, Nottingham, instead of a private Catholic high school, which they hated. I started to walk to school with Dan and his older sister, and met them at the intersection of Scottholm Boulevard and Scott Ave. From there we would walk down the street, cross Genesee Street, walk along Genesee Park Drive, along the curve to Ferris Ave. Left on Ferris, fifty yards, and then a right on Salt Springs. A couple hundred feet up the street was Our Lady of Solace, at the corner of Salt Springs and East Ave.

I learned to walk very quickly in these days. Dan was always much taller than me—the tallest in our class, even in high school. So, walking with him, and his older sister, who was the same height as Dan, I had to walk quickly or be left behind. Ain't no pity for the slow in Syracuse.

Bruce's destruction had also begun to take a more linear descent. The disobeying my parents and partying, he now took to a new level. He started to run with other guys in school—worse than the bad influences in Catholic school, and with new connections for drugs. When he hooked up with these other guys' older brothers, that brought new troubles and new connections. The drinking age was still eighteen, so access to alcohol was much easier.

Bruce was either dealing or buying drugs over the phone with this guy named S. I remember his conversations. As I got older and became more street-savvy, his cryptic talk became more understandable. My parents had no idea that he was hanging out and getting high with the neighbor's daughter and friends up in her garage loft.

The school year went along as usual: hang with Dan after school as much as possible, to avoid Bruce, and when home, just try not to be in the same room with him. I stayed in my room and read as much as I could, trying not to listen through my bedroom door to the fighting on an almost-nightly basis: about his coming home late, not doing homework, not knowing where he was. It was the same thing over and over. Maybe it involved a different person, or place, but it was all the same. Nights were battlegrounds, and I did my best to avoid them. Homework was near impossible for me. I did the best I could.

Everyone in my family had stress and it permeated all the way down to me. *This is not how families are supposed to be,* I used to think. But no matter how hard I tried to avoid the confrontations, their noise would always find me. I was in constant fight-or-flight mode, but with no one to fight except myself.

Bruce did everything he could to push my parents' buttons, and nothing they said to him seemed to make a difference. His attitude and actions did not change, but instead got worse. My fear and anxiety rose daily, making it hard to sleep, and sometimes hard to eat. I had to keep to a certain routine, no matter what. Bruce dictated how I would live, whether he knew it or not.

At this time, my sister was outside of the house quite a bit, spending time at the playhouse, writing as much as she could, and working. Christmas came and went, Bruce still ruling the homestead with his actions, stealing money from my parents and sister for drugs and alcohol.

Having a sibling who is in constant trouble means sometimes the anger from the parents rolls onto the other children, whether they did anything to warrant it or not. A few times, my parents blew a gasket over something minor with me, or my brother or sister, and way overreacted. But that's what happens when emotions and feelings bleed over: sometimes the wrong people get the heat.

I didn't understand this until I went back and thought about it, but by then the damage had been done. My siblings and I had to wade through constant pools of shit, and it was stressful and tiring. The bad times outweighed the good times, and that sucks more than anything.

In the spring, my sister asked me if I wanted to read a high school book, and I said sure. She was curious about my reading aptitude after the play. We sat on our front porch steps, her on the top step and me between her legs on the bottom step. The book she chose was actually a play, and it was no ordinary play: *The Glass Menagerie* by Tennessee Williams.

Now, Tennessee does not write happy, cheery plays full of love and hope. Nope, just the opposite. My sister could have picked a play with a few less traumas, considering the caseload we were both carrying at home.

Then my sister volunteered my brother and myself for *Jesus Chris Superstar.* She presented the info so that it sounded like a good idea, plus neither of us wanted to be in the house with Bruce. He could be downright scary. Now, with my mom working, no one but Bruce would be home after school, if he decided to show up. My brother and I would go home, change, do homework, eat quickly, and then walk the half-hour to the playhouse. We would do rehearsal, and my dad or cousin would pick us up after. More late nights.

But in *Jesus Christ Superstar,* neither my brother nor I had a speaking role. We were part of the chorus and the group of kids that follow Jesus around, until he runs into his hammer and nail problem.

It was a fine production. This was a few months after the Iran hostage situation, so they used that premise in the opening scene. Once the crowd was seated, a bunch of us kids scattered along the aisles. Once the house went black, there were a few seconds of silence and then *Boom!* The bass and guitar started their opening riffs; the music exceptionally loud for effect. Once the music was rolling, strobe lights started going off onstage. Men with masked faces, armed with rifles and shotguns (real, unloaded and firing pins removed), herded people onstage, replicating a hostage takeover. The hostages (cast members) were rounded up, from the audience onto the stage—complete with pushing, shoving, and semi-violent altercations between hostage and hostage-taker. The hostages were then taken offstage.

The strobe light faded and a back light faded in, center stage, about ten feet off the ground. As the stage light softened, we kids began to make our way up the aisles to center stage. The image of the man playing Jesus came into focus: he was on the cross, about ten feet off the ground, looking down. The band switched gears and the music was softer, warmer, as the kids reached center stage, looking up at the cross. Fade to black.

The production ran until April. I remember on one of the last nights, I was in the crowd when we started and there was an old lady next to me. She had about twenty crucifixes around her neck. When I sat down, she looked at me as though she had just won the lottery. She was a grandma and I was hungry, wondering if she had any crackers in that purse of hers. I bet she did.

Spring was on the way in central New York. The flowers gave it away. Luckily, Bruce was not around much, mostly off with his running partners. That also meant there was potential for late night trauma if he came home fucked up.

At the school spring carnival, held in the gym, I spent all my money, so I went home to find some more. I ended up taking five bucks from Bruce's paper route money. Bruce found out, and told my parents, and they knew it was me. My punishment was to get up that Monday morning, and all the other mornings that week, and deliver Bruce's paper route.

I was up at 5:30 on Monday morning. I had only ever been up that early to go fishing. After the first two days, I pretty much did the whole route by myself, as he watched. Sometimes he would send me down the street to deliver to a lone house, and I'd look up and he'd be gone, around the corner and on his way, expecting me to hurry and catch up. By Thursday, I was delivering every paper by myself, and Bruce would just head home without me.

That Saturday morning, I got home from delivering and went in my room and back to sleep. When I woke up about an hour later, it was threatening rain. I puttered around the house, the pockets of cold keeping me inside.

That afternoon, I realized I had Bruce's newspaper bag in my room. Bruce delivered only morning papers, Monday through Saturday; the Sunday paper was actually delivered by someone else. I did not want possession of that bag come Monday morning, or Bruce would come in and wake me up at 5:30 a.m.

I grabbed the bag and went upstairs to his room, which was right above my and my other brother's room. The only people home were me, Bruce, and my dad, who was in the living room watching TV.

I brought the bag up and walked down the hall. The door was cracked and I knocked on it, afraid to walk in. I pushed open the door and Bruce was on his bed.

"What?"

I came in, showed him the bag, and threw it on the chair in his room.

He looked at me, then told me to come in and close the door.

He instructed me to get on my knees, and then he made me perform on him.

And then he told me to get out. I quickly got to my feet and left, went back down to my room, and shut the door, awash in fear and anger.

I was seven. Bruce was thirteen.

I stayed in my room until dinner. I tried to read, but I could not focus on the words. I put on the radio, but just kept switching the station. Nothing felt good, or right. I sat there and asked myself what I was going to do. I was very afraid. The weight of the fear—to this day, I still cannot completely explain. I did not know what to do.

My brother, mother, and cousin all came home over the next few hours. I did not go out to see them; I just stayed in my room. My mom called me for dinner and I could not go out. But I didn't want to raise suspicion, so I slunk out of my room to the dining room. I took my seat—back to the window, to the right of my dad, and right across the table from Bruce Jr. I did not lift my eyes from my plate, nor did I make a sound. I was afraid to exist.

I ate out of instinct, nothing more. I felt that any movement or sound would light the bomb known as Bruce Jr. Everything seemed to be moving in slow-motion, and the dialogue seemed scripted. I finished my meal and went right back to my room. I skipped dessert that night, and many nights after. I did not want to spend a single second more than I had to at that table.

When I took my plate to the sink, I removed a steak knife from the drawer and put it in my pocket. In my room, I slid the knife under my mattress, and switched the radio on. I did not want to hear what was happening on the other side of the door. I just lay in my bed in a ball.

The night passed quickly. The next thing I knew, my brother was in the room getting ready for bed.

"Can I turn the light off?" he asked as he walked toward the door.

"No, go ahead, if I read I'll turn the reading lamp on, so I don't wake you up."

The light went out and my brother climbed into bed. He was asleep in minutes, lucky bastard. I was wide awake and my mind was racing so fast, I could not fully comprehend it. I knew what Bruce had done was very wrong and I knew that he would be in major trouble if anyone found out.

And that was part of the fear: if someone found out. What would he do to me if someone found out he assaulted me? What would he do to the person?

I lay awake for hours, listening to the sounds in my house.

I listened to my cousin go into her and my sister's room, across the hall from me and my brother. I heard Bruce go upstairs, and then my parents, sometime later.

When finally, the house was quiet and I was the only one up, I started to cry, with my face buried in my pillow so my brother would not hear me.

What did he do to me? Why? Did I deserve it? Was it the money I stole? Did I do something wrong? Who can I tell? How? What will happen if I tell? Can my parents help? My cousin? My sister? My brother? The cops? Dan? Garrett? What the fuck am I supposed to do?

I cried until there was nothing left. After running out of tears, I just lay there processing these questions through my head, one after another. *Who can help? Will they? Can they?* I ran those thoughts through my head over and over.

I must have fallen asleep, because my eyes flew open at 5:15 a.m. My mind was immediately moving at a thousand miles an hour; I had never felt this way before. The same questions kept flying through my mind: *What if, what if, and what if?*

It was 5:30 a.m. and I did not hear Bruce's alarm go off.

Oh fuck, is there a problem? Is he home? Why is he deviating from his pattern?

I reached down and put my hand under my mattress, grabbed the steak knife that I'd put there the night before. I was afraid Bruce was about to burst through the door and get me.

It took me a few minutes to remember it was Sunday. I relaxed, a little. He was not up because he didn't have to be. It took a while to let the steak knife go and relax.

That was another dreary day, so no outside activities. I spent the entire day, except for meals, in my room—for the first and only time in my life. I left for meals and the bathroom. I was too afraid to do anything else.

I realized that day that Bruce had won, and I had lost. Everything, whatever everything was, he won it. I could never shake that feeling. It left me defeated and scared. All of my confidence and self-esteem dissolved.

At nighttime, my brother came into the room to read. We

each sat in our beds, above the covers, and read. He eventually killed the lights and went to sleep.

I lay awake the whole night this time. I kept asking myself the same questions, over and over—a complete and constant grind on my mind, the whole night.

What if? What if? What if?

Suddenly, there was a blast of music and I turned over in my bed and reached for the steak knife. It was 5:30 a.m. I had been awake the whole night and Bruce's alarm had just gone off.

I heard him get up and get dressed. When he was walking down the stairs toward my room, I was white-knuckled, with the steak knife in my hand, shaking.

I would now have to pay attention to all of Bruce's movements. I knew when he was asleep, and when he got up. I knew when he stumbled in late and argued with my parents.

I now had no time to spend thinking about what I wanted to be when I grew up. I was now thinking about whether I would be alive to see my tenth birthday.

That Monday morning, I got up and got ready for school. I got my bowl of cereal and ate it in front of Jane Pauley. I felt haunted —nervous and scared. Bruce went along with his usual morning business, ignoring me unless I was useful, which was not out of the ordinary. Bruce and my sister left, separately, and then I followed. The air was fresh after a day of rain, still a little wet.

As I rounded the corner on Scottholm, I saw Dan and his sister enter the intersection. I picked up my pace a little, then slowed a little to make sure I did not look hurried. I was extremely self-conscious of how I appeared to others; I did not want to show that anything was wrong.

I gave my usual greeting to the two of them and we started the walk down Scott Ave. toward school. Dan asked me about my weekend, I gave a starched reply and asked about his. We both had nothing going on, with a wet weekend.

Neither Dan nor his sister asked me what really happened

that weekend—how could they?

So, it was right then and there, as we approached Genesee Street, that I decided to never tell anyone what had happened to me. Since I felt like I had no safe place to go, no one I could tell that could 100 percent guarantee me I was and would be safe, I was going to keep the sexual assault by my brother Bruce quiet.

I created an arbitrary mark, which neither Dan nor his sister knew about. Once we crossed the middle of Genesee Street, there was no going back. My Rubicon was declared.

A man gets tied up to the ground
He gives the world its saddest sound
Its saddest sound.[3]

About the time *Jesus Christ Superstar* ended, Salt Springs baseball started again. I was a horrible ball player, but I truly enjoyed being on the team with Garrett and Dan. It gave me something to do and got me out of the house, away from Bruce. It was also at this time that I was asked to reprise my role as Theo in a production of *Pippin* at a local high school. I said I would do it, because, if I am being completely honest, I really enjoyed the applause. So I was going to school, with baseball practice a few nights a week, and games on the weekend; play practice was after baseball practice. I was rather busy, and I liked it.

But things were beginning to crumble. What I did not know was how long it would take for it to all fall apart. On the second night of the play, I completely missed my cue and was given a chaperone after that. Her iced tea smelled like whiskey because it was. In the fourth show I completely flubbed a line, and I could not believe it. I had about fifteen lines in the whole show, and I knew them by heart.

But my mind was somewhere else. It would always be somewhere else, from that point forward. My mind and my body would almost never be in the same place.

The night the show ended, I remember finishing the last performance, packing my costume, my pretend pet duck, and my script into my gray backpack, not saying a word to anyone, and just walking out of the school. I got into my dad's car and went home. I took the backpack and threw it in the back of my closet. I would not set foot on a theatrical stage again until 2004. I never acted again.

Life at home was getting more and more miserable. Not only was I living in fear, but Bruce was acting out more and more: coming home late, or not at all, and arguing with my parents on the daily.

I did everything I could to make sure I was not home alone with Bruce. Luckily, he didn't always come home after high school. That allowed me to get home, change, and get out of the house as fast as I could. Not only was I afraid of him doing what he did to me again—I was afraid that he might ask if I had told anyone or was thinking of it. It occurred to me that not even our German shepherd could save me, because he would not really recognize the harm from someone in the family until it was too late. This fear was like an ever-present ache, wearing me down a little at a time. A slow, internal chiseling away of everything I was as a person.

School ended and summer arrived. Unfortunately, there were no lazy days of sleeping in for me—I had to keep track of Bruce's movements. I was still lying in bed at night, running through all the scenarios of who I might tell, and the math just never worked. I never found a solution that felt like it would keep me safe, and I didn't believe any institution could help me either. Sometimes I slept, but woke up right before his alarm at 5:30. Sometimes I didn't sleep at all.

Bruce gave up the paper route that summer. There was probably more money to be made on the street, dealing drugs or stealing. Plus, the route interfered with his late hours and lifestyle of no responsibilities. I spent my time over at Dan's and playing with other kids in the neighborhood, out of the house as much as I could be. Sometimes, my cousin C would drop me off at Garrett's and I'd spend my days there. My mom was back to working as a teacher full-time but had her summers free.

I tried my best to avoid the chaos of home, but that isn't so easy when you're nine years old. I certainly did not have the freedom that my sister had. She was gone a lot, hanging out with older people, college students and professionals. She found people that she could write with and bounce ideas off of. She hadn't been getting anything like that in high school.

The chaos always started after dark. Whatever Bruce did usually followed him home and the fireworks would soon follow. My parents spent a lot of time and energy trying to change Bruce. Unfortunately, they were totally unqualified to take something like that on. No unlicensed health professional is. We tried individual counseling and family counseling, but nothing worked.

The summer went by and nothing out of the ordinary happened, other than an escalation of Bruce's erratic and shitty behavior: more threats of violence, verbal brawls with my parents. He became more aggressive and intimidating.

I skinned my knees, played ball, and played a good deal of D&D with my other brother. We would close our door, turn off the main light, and whisper so we could play late into the night. I liked this, because I hated lying in bed and wondering what would happen to me. It was a great distraction and allowed my mind to wander, and be free.

I also knew if Bruce was going to come and get me, it was better that I was awake, with a fighting chance.

CHAPTER 4

Fourth grade started like every other school year, except I got a morning paper route. I now had to be up and out of the house at 5:30 a.m., no matter the weather. I would do the route, come home and clean up, get changed, eat, and then go meet Dan and his older sister for our walk to Solace.

It was an adjustment, but it wasn't like I was sleeping anyway. It took some getting used to, especially because the nights were becoming ever more raucous. Bruce's fighting, stealing, drinking, drugging was getting louder, bigger, more frightful, more chaotic. Everything just got dialed up to 1,000. It was weird to have a front-row seat to Bruce's destruction and not know why it was happening. I would later have front-row seats to my own and not understand it either.

The next summer, we had a family reunion in Massachusetts to celebrate my grandparents' fiftieth wedding anniversary. It was a fun time, spending time with relatives and meeting friends of my grandparents that I'd never met; most of the men were veterans of World War II.

This was the first time I heard a dirty joke, which I did not know was dirty at the time. I was sitting in the kitchen with the older male group, who were mixing drinks and laughing about various things. My father and grandfather were both in the room, and this one man was just getting to the climax of his joke—when in walked my mom. The next words from his mouth made my mom sputter—at my dad, then her dad—and I was told to leave the kitchen, just as he was getting to the punchline. I still do not know what happened on that fucking farm.

Another highlight was witnessing my cousin D and Bruce getting caught drinking. They were mixing booze into their sodas on the sly. Things became apparent to the older set when Bruce tried to push himself up on one of those old ashtray stands, the bronze-looking ones with a large ashtray. Needless to say, it could not hold his weight and it went flying. He and my cousin then fell into each other, and Bruce passed out on a table full of food.

My parents pulled us out of there real quick—and they were pissed. My cousin was my aunt and uncle's problem. This might have been written off as high school hijinks, but it had passed the "kids will be kids" stage months before we showed up there.

Bruce at my grandparents in Massachusetts. When I showed
my therapist this picture, she had never seen him, she said he
looked "angry". That is how he always looked I remarked.

Bruce was on a tear, fighting with my parents almost nightly in the kitchen. Then, suddenly, I came home one day to find my dad was in the hospital—the psychiatric ward, to be exact.

I would later come to find out that when my dad was young, he had a very strong relationship with his grandmother, Bammy, his mom's mom. When she passed away my dad was around nine years old and he took a chair, placed it in a corner, and stared at the wall for two weeks.

My father was suffering from undiagnosed depression. And in the early 1950s, no one really knew what depression was or how to cure it. I can only imagine my grandmother at this time, telling him to "just stop your nonsense right now, time to get over it." My grandmother couldn't muster up empathy for a dying person at gunpoint.

From my perspective, my father's general mood hadn't seemed to indicate that he was suffering from depression. But my dad was in the hospital for a couple weeks, and I went to visit him with my other brother and mom. It was like my dad was nine and he was in the chair facing the wall all over again. I was so scared for him, and for us. I did not want to see my dad sick, and I was scared he would never get out and Bruce would rule the house.

Bruce took full advantage of my dad being gone, and ramped up his asshole antics. He and my mom got into it one night and he punched my mom in the stomach. As she doubled over, my cousin C stepped in and got in between Bruce and my mom. Bruce did nothing to my cousin—not out of respect, but because she has four brothers, and if they found out Bruce did anything to her, it would be game fucking over.

After two weeks on antidepressants my dad was out of the hospital and back to his normal self. He found out Bruce hit my mom, though, and he was not happy. We had a family meeting in the living room and my dad laid down the law, more for Bruce than the rest of us. But Bruce exploded and an argument ensued between him and my dad. He stormed off, was gone for about thirty seconds, and came storming back toward the living room.

In the doorway, he raised a twelve-gauge shotgun, choked it, and pointed it right at my dad. My mother gasped and I could see my sister white-knuckle the couch with her left fist.

My sister, my brother, and I were on the couch. Next to me on the ground was a bike chain that had randomly been left in the living room—one of the old locks, chain link with a blue plastic cover, with the combination lock attached to the chain itself.

It ran through my mind to grab that chain and throw it at Bruce, hoping to hit the shotgun pointed at my dad. That thought went out of my head quickly, though—because if I fucked up, we could all literally be dead. Shotguns typically hold five shells, and there were five of us in the room.

My father remained cool as a fucking cucumber. He looked at Bruce and told him he was making a mistake and that his actions would ruin the rest of his life. Bruce told him to go fuck himself.

My father looked at him, lowered his head a little, looked at him over his glasses, and turned back to the newspaper that was in his lap. Bruce stayed there for a few seconds, which seemed like years, with the shotgun still trained on my dad. And then Bruce quickly retreated and left the house.

My dad got up, locked the front and back door. He went and found the shotgun, unloaded it, then took the firing pins out of all the weapons in the house.

Bruce showed back up that night. He crawled in through our kitchen window, drunk as fuck, and would not leave the house.

He wandered upstairs to his room, and my dad got up and went out the front door. Two minutes later he returned with our neighbor PD in tow. Both of them looked ready for business and went upstairs. My father could be heard loudly telling Bruce he had to leave. Bruce told my dad and PD to go fuck right off.

From what I'm told, they both looked at each other, and then grabbed Bruce by his head and arms and proceeded to throw him down the long hall to his room. Bruce made the mistake of fighting back, in his drunken state, and they threw

Bruce half through the wall. My dad got Bruce on the ground and pinned his arm behind his back. Bruce screamed in pain and yelled that my dad was hurting him. My dad did not give a fuck.

My dad called down to my mom to call the police. Bruce told my dad that if he gave him fifty dollars he would never see him again and not have to worry. My dad retorted, "So you can go out and buy drugs!" He also reminded Bruce that he had already stolen my mom's engagement ring and sold that, so he did not think any more assets needed to be released at this juncture.

The police showed up, and they cuffed Bruce and took him away. It was not yet Thanksgiving of fourth grade.

That Monday morning, when I got back from my paper route, my sister, brother, and I all went off to our respective schools, and my parents went to the Syracuse courthouse. Once there, they would file what is known as a PINS petition, Person in Need of Supervision. My parents were taking legal steps to have Bruce removed from the house. He would no longer be allowed to live with us, or visit without permission. Basically, my parents were kicking him out and he was going to be placed in a halfway house.

With fourth grade so far a disaster, I went on a tear. If there was a fuck to give about being a good student, it was not in my pocket. With so much havoc being wreaked at home, I started causing havoc in my own world: aggressively acting out toward everyone, especially fellow students. I became a dick to everyone I encountered, including Dan and Garrett, lashing out at everyone and everything.

I was angry and I did not know why. I wanted the world to know I was angry, but I did not want to tell them why, or that I needed help. I was drowning in my own pool of anger, not knowing how to swim, or even if I would survive. I would end up getting detention in school about forty or fifty times over the next three-year period.

But at least with Bruce gone, things calmed down quite a bit in the house. For the foreseeable future, Bruce was not allowed in the house, and if I saw him I was to call my mom or dad, or the police if they could not be reached. Trust me when I say that it had always been in the back of my mind to call the cops. I was just too scared to do it. But I also did not know if they would help, so taking the chance wasn't worth it, with the threat of setting Bruce off and having him come for me. I secretly carried his felony with me at all times.

My parents had been able to remove Bruce, which I had been too scared to try myself. Courage is hard to find at that age, under those circumstances. Any sense of normalcy or calm was extremely hard to find. As much as I tried and no matter how tough I thought I was, I could never pick up that phone to help myself. I was fearful of what could have gone wrong if I did— that I could have gotten family members hurt, or even killed. I was trapped.

Christmas day, Bruce was living in a halfway house. We waited for him to be released from his house and picked him up, then went home to open presents. Needless to say, that Christmas sucked. Now we were being held hostage not by his presence, but by his absence.

Bruce's birthday was December 26, so no matter how it started, the holiday always just ended up turning into shit. My mom's birthday was next, on the 27th, and my parents' anniversary on the 29th. All of that was usually interrupted by Bruce's exploits and whatever he happened to drag home that day.

I cannot really say when I had a normal, free Christmas. Probably not until high school, and even then a cloud always hung over the day. My first real Christmas celebration probably didn't happen until I had my own family.

School started back up, and I was still pretty much being a jerk to everyone, taking out my anger and pain out on everyone else, instead of getting help. The second half of the school year went along without Bruce, but we could not escape his shadow. My parents still worried about him and what he was going through, and neglected me and my siblings in the house.

Bruce finally got released from the halfway house by the court, and allowed back in our home, but he had to go to night school. That was great for me because he wouldn't be home when I got home and he wouldn't get there until after 7 p.m., when everyone else was home.

When the summer started, he got back together with his old running partners, people he did drugs and committed crimes with in the streets. One night, he was out drinking with his friends and ended up running across one of Syracuse's police officers. I guess the cops rolled up, everyone bolted, and Bruce got grabbed. Apparently, that angered Bruce and he took a swing at the cop. Welcome to the big time!

My parents were floored. This was not getting caught drinking with some buddies; he had just stepped it up to felony assault of a police officer. That's not something you can usually just walk away from, even if it is a first offense. But Bruce was eventually able to avoid the whole matter and not have to pay for hitting the officer at all—at least not until much later.

During this time, if you got caught committing certain offenses in the civilian world, they would accept you into the military in lieu of going through the judicial system. Instead of Bruce being prosecuted for punching a police officer with a closed fist, and whatever other offense may have been attributed to his actions that night, my brother—who sexually assaulted me, physically assaulted my family, and pointed a loaded shotgun at my father—was being accepted into the United States Marine Corps.

My parents and the school district made a plan for Bruce to finish up his schoolwork and get his GED, which he would need to be accepted into the Marine Corp. I was relieved that after that, Bruce would not be around anymore; I had been living on pins and needles (literally, with the knife under my mattress) since that Saturday in third grade. It was frightening and exhausting. During the interim, Bruce was in the house and I did everything possible to avoid him. I was slowly giving up my childhood, so I could stay alive.

It had become harder and harder to plan and be aware of Bruce's movements, and keep track of my own world. I was multitasking my way through life, and one of my tasks was making sure I didn't die. The idea of not having to watch my back and be careful of every move I made in the house was a relief.

On Father's Day in fourth grade—after a Knights of Columbus picnic, then after making my grandmother and himself a nightcap—my mom's dad had a heart attack and passed away, with his wife of fifty years at his side. He was dead within two minutes; there was no ambulance to call. My parents woke me up at 4 a.m. All the house lights were on and bags were being packed.

My grandfather held not only a special place in our family, but a special place in American history, for he was a soldier in the Ghost Army. The 23rd Headquarters Special Troops was a brand-new support group created during World War II to help deceive the Axis Powers into believing operations were or were not being carried out by the Allied troops. My grandfather, being a graduate of Princeton and having military experience, was a prime candidate for this type of work. He went away to war in 1941 and ended up being one of the last soldiers to help wind the unit down; to this day, most of what he did is still classified by the military. My family members revered him for this job, even though they didn't know much about it.

The funeral had all the usual suspects: old couples waiting for their turn, cousins, aunts, and uncles greeting each other again, most of whom I would never see again. Bruce was not permitted to go to the funeral. I truthfully do not think he cared, or understood why he should care. The summer went on as usual: hang out with Garrett and Dan during the day and play kick the can at night. Bruce went to jail for a little while and then another halfway house. He still had some time away before the Marine plan was to be put into action. For a little while, I felt safe. It would not last long.

That summer I learned to ride my bike. All the kids came out for bike riding, kickball, soccer, baseball, Frisbee. It was an active neighborhood, in spite of my criminal brother. With Bruce gone, the only thing that took physical abuse that summer was my garage door, and my bike. Also, at the beginning of summer, my cousin C moved out. I could not blame her one bit—it had been nothing but chaos since she arrived, none of it her fault. She ended up moving across town about ten minutes away, and she still worked for the same organization for the developmentally disabled. C would occasionally stop by and play catch with me, with a cigarette in her hand.

CHAPTER 5

In about mid-October of fifth grade, Bruce was moving back into the house soon. One early evening the doorbell rang and our front door was opened. Rip was going nuts.

My cousin C popped in with a little boy, about two or three years younger than me. She looked out of sorts, and appeared very frantic. She came in and closed the door behind her.

I was sitting on the couch, looking at her and this little boy. Rip gave out a few more barks and sniffed the little boy's feet, delighting and frightening him at the same time.

My cousin grabbed my dad, and my mom followed them out to the kitchen. Along the way, they placed the boy at the head of the dining room table, in my dad's chair.

I heard voices talking, low but fast. After a minute or two, my dad came walking out of the dining room with a set of keys in one hand and a twelve-inch flashlight in the other. He opened the front door and walked out without saying a word.

By now I knew something was very wrong. My cousin looked scared and my dad was moving with purpose.

My mom called me into the kitchen, where I found her, my cousin, and this boy, who I'll call Jim. My mom said, "Jim's going to spend the night with us and sleep in your room."

"Okay," I responded and I looked at Jim and smiled. He looked exhausted, and very frazzled. I don't think he understood what was going on, but neither did I yet.

"Maybe you can go get something from your room for you guys to play with," my mom said. I looked at her and nodded.

In my room I found a box, sitting in front of my discarded backpack. It held a track that had a truck chassis on it, which traveled around, picking up different things, transporting them, and then dumping them. I'd gotten it a couple of Christmases earlier.

I grabbed the box and turned around. Jim was standing there, waiting patiently. I told him to follow me and we walked out to the dining room table. I placed the box on the table, where Bruce usually sat, and took a seat. I let Jim crawl into my dad's chair at the head of the table. We little people did not usually get such privileges, and he looked like he needed it.

I opened the box and started to remove the pieces, as my mom walked out with a glass of milk and some crackers for Jim. She asked if I wanted anything and I said I was fine. I was just trying to piece together what was going on. My cousin seemed amped; I had never seen her like this. She and my mom stayed in the kitchen and talked in hushed tones.

After five minutes or so, my dad came back through the front door. He shook off the cold and walked to the kitchen, where my mom and cousin were still talking quietly. I was straining to hear what they were saying, while also trying to keep Jim occupied, and answering his questions. He was attempting to help put the track together, but was more interested in the crackers and milk.

I finally got it set up and handed the chassis over to Jim, showing him where to turn it on. He hit the switch and a small smile flashed on his face. I pointed to where he needed to set it down, and he followed, placing it on the track. Off it went, picking up the dump truck shell, off to get the marbles.

Without looking up, Jim blurted out, "My dad gets angry and hits things."

I froze and just looked at the table for a few seconds. My dad spanked me, but that was not what Jim was talking about.

I looked up at him and he had this matter-of-fact look on his face. He did not seem to realize the trouble in his statement. Neither did I at the time, not really.

Jim and I played there for a couple hours, with my mom and C eventually sitting at the table with us. My dad went to the living room to watch TV, but he was acting funny, like something was wrong. I couldn't put my finger on what. He kept the flashlight within arm's reach. Every once in a while he got up and looked out the bay window through the curtains, like he does when snow is falling. My father's "tell" are his sighs; I just did not know what had gotten him so amped up.

After a while, my cousin took Jim into my room and tucked him into the spare bed. She stayed and read him a few stories. I still had all the books that I used to read when the chaos outside reigned. They helped protect me a lot when I was younger, and it was good to see they were now providing some comfort for someone else.

After a half hour, around 10 p.m., I went to bed—later than usual, due to the special circumstances, my mom said. Jim was already asleep, good for him.

I crawled into bed and put the radio on quietly: the sweet sounds of Kansas's "Carry on Wayward Son." I had my alarm set for my morning papers, but I pulled it close to my head, so I could get to it quicker and not wake Jim. My brother did not arrive home until later that night and my dad filled him in. In high school, my brother spent a lot of time doing after-school activities, so he was not around all that much.

I lay there for a little while and looked at Jim. I still did not know what was going on, or what it was like where he lived, but he had seemed scared. It was late, almost 11, but I was used to late nights.

Sometimes I got into bed and fell right to sleep, but other times my brain would be taken over by negative thoughts of specific people or events. They were not really based in truth, and I did not know where the thoughts came from, or why. They would just appear, and then disappear, like visual drive-bys.

My brain was beginning to start to think on its own. It would pick a subject and thrust it into my present mental being. These were the beginning stages of me being held captive by my own brain.

BOOM! Suddenly a loud, thunderous slam shook the house and the doorbell rang. Rip started barking furiously, and I could tell from the snarls that he wanted something, or someone. I heard a bunch more commotion and yelling and several more loud bangs, and sat up in bed.

My eyes were well adjusted to the dark. Jim was still asleep. I could see his chest move a little. I heard yelling out in the living room. My dad, my cousin, and my mom were all yelling but I couldn't really make out the words.

I then heard my mom yell "BRUCE!"—once, then again. There was a distinct way my mom would say my dad's name, versus my brother's name. Her tone suggested she was yelling at my dad. My mom's sense of displeasure or fear could be gauged by the number of times and the tone in which she said my dad's first name. Anything more than two "Bruce's" and my dad knew he was in trouble, most likely for saying something in front of us kids. But a third "Bruce" meant there was trouble, and my pop was coming loaded for who or whatever was causing the trouble. They had better hope their prayers are up to date.

Even though I did not know what was truly happening on the other side of the door, I knew it was dangerous. My time around Bruce had made me highly attuned to bad situations. I told myself that if Mom reached three or more Bruce's, or I heard yelling and no Rip, I was putting on clothes, waking Jim, opening the window to the driveway, and going out. It was a drop of a couple feet to the driveway, and fifteen feet to my neighbor's side door. He was well aware of my family's problems and would have called the cops and released his dogs before he "batted" up and went to help my dad. His two golden retriever field dogs were voice- and whistle-controlled. One, the female, loved my dad so much that when she saw him daily, she would pee on his foot. Whatever my dad was dealing with, that dog would have gone right to his side.

I laid waiting for my cue, listening, but didn't hear any more loud noises, just murmuring that I could tell was my mom. I also heard a lighter, which meant one of them was lighting a cigarette. *Coast is clear?*

At about five minutes after five, I sprang awake. I looked

over at the spare bed, but Jim was gone. My alarm went off and I hit it quick, took a deep breath, and got out of bed. When I opened my door, Rip was asleep outside my room, which was very unusual. I went to the bathroom, then back to my room. The house was dead quiet, except for a faint noise coming from the living room.

I got dressed and crept out of my room, stepping over Rip. He quickly joined me at my side, and through the dining room. The track was still set up, just how we'd left it. No lights were on. The living room was dark.

My dad was not sitting in his chair, but when I entered the living room I could see the red glow of his cigarette as he inhaled. He was sitting at the end of the couch, in the dark.

"Good morning," he said in a low, expressionless voice.

"Good morning," I responded. "Where's Jim?"

"He's with social services, and your cousin is back at home." I waited for a second to let my dad pause and gather himself before he spoke again. "The guy your cousin was dating came home drunk last night, and got physical and scared her. She grabbed Jim and came over here. The guy came over and wanted to get in to see Jim and C. I was not going to let that happen."

My dad paused for a second, then took another drag, the red glow lighting his face and glasses. "He tried to force his way in. Your mother called the cops and finally he was picked up a few hours ago. C went home and Jim was given over to child services, since C is not the legal guardian."

I stood there absorbing the information; I was truly scared for my cousin and this boy. I did not want to see either of them hurt.

"Look," my father blurted, "I don't know how long this guy will be kept in jail, if at all. While you're on your route, if you see a suspicious man you've never seen before, or there is a car following you, run. Hit the bushes and make your way back here. If you see someone fishy and can't run, ring the doorbell of the house you're at. Throw something through a window if you have to."

I told him I would, then turned and walked back to my room. I had a small wooden box with a picture of four playing cards on top; one of each suit. It was handmade by my grandfather, my mom's dad, and given to me upon his death. I reached inside and pulled out my pocket knife, put it in my pocket, and left.

I walked back to the living room with the knife in my pocket and my newspaper bag. I walked toward the front door. A large cardboard box with clothes for Goodwill had been sitting in the hall for about two weeks before this incident. I pushed it aside to find our white, wooden front door had a panel that had been entirely kicked in.

I stepped out onto the porch and closed the door behind me, wondering what the rest of the day would bring. The week? The month?

Situations like this one added to my already intense anxiety. My symptoms at this time included increased heart rate, altered breath, and sweating. They led to outbursts in school and general confusion. As I grew, my general anxiety baseline rose and my fight-or-flight responses became more frequent.

Now I know that I was incapable of processing the emotions I was having at the time and did not understand where they came from. At this time, I already had a hard time sleeping and was just beginning a swing into mental self-destruction; now another thing had been added to my plate. I felt like all I did was think of adult things, instead of being a kid.

About two weeks later, Garrett's parents and my parents ended up at Friendly's for ice cream. C was there, and offered to give me and Garrett a ride home.

As we left, my dad grabbed my arm and pulled me down so my ear was close to his mouth. "Make sure you're the first one in the house. Behind the desk there's a loaded twelve-gauge. Take it upstairs and put it on my bed, then pull the covers over it." I stood up, looked down at him, and nodded in agreement, despite this being not part of the job description for an eleven-year-old boy.

When we got home, I bolted out of the car, telling Garrett I needed to let Rip out because it had been awhile. I ran up the sidewalk, threw my key in the lock, and went in. Rip greeted me at the door and was all over me, but I pushed by him and went directly to the desk. There was the shotgun, with its top facing out, ready to aim.

I quickly grabbed it and swung it up, double-checking that the safety was on. Then I walked quickly up to my parents' room, where I placed the weapon on the bed and pulled the covers over it.

Downstairs, I heard Garrett coming in and quickly let Rip out, then walked back into the kitchen, where I was met by Garrett.

"What happened to the door?"

My father was having a hard time getting the right-size door—metal this time. I gave Garrett the basic rundown of what had happened. He knew my cousin well, and was very surprised to hear what I had to say.

It was fifth grade. We were both surprised.

I was still acting out in school, but not as much as the year before. Now I tried at act funny, instead of mean.

Bruce was completing his GED and had started physical exercise under my dad's tutelage. The Marines provide you with a sheet of physical exercises, including running times, which a recruit is strongly suggested to master. Bruce was in for a rude awakening. He was more athletic than our other brother, but his last physical exercise had been running from and punching a policeman.

But Bruce kept his head down and did what he was told. He knew he had just gotten a new lease on life, which was guaranteed by my father's signature to the United States Marine Corps, since Bruce was only seventeen. He also knew that circumstances could change very quickly and those assault charges could land him right in prison, not jail. His GED class ran until 8 p.m. at night, so my time around him was limited. Usually, he was just getting up when I would be on my way to meet Dan and his older sister for our walk to school, and he wouldn't be home after school.

I avoided him as much as possible and did everything I could not to be in the same room with him alone. If we were in the living room watching TV, and someone walked out and left the two of us alone, I would get up and leave the room, and come back later when someone else was there. No one noticed this because no one wanted to be near Bruce.

My sleep had become more disjointed. I was finding it harder to fall asleep, and when I woke up early sometimes, at 3 or 4, I could not get back to sleep. I would just start to run the same thoughts and scenes through my head, over and over again for no real reason. Scenes of my life would play over and over, leaving me wondering why my brain was running these short films in my head. These thoughts took up so much of the space of what a normal kid would be thinking. The more you think like an adult, about safety and fears, the less you think about being a kid.

I kept to myself and to my room as much as possible. I read, but with less enthusiasm than before. I listened to the radio all the time, always listening to see if someone would write a song I knew, without ever hearing the words before. Was someone able to write something about my life while never having met me? Music, songs were a support for me.

The school year moved along and for the time being, everything was relatively smooth. Bruce was getting his GED and working out. My sister was spending all her time out of the house either with friends, or at the playhouse. My other brother would just read or watch TV. We didn't play any D&D at this time because neither of us wanted Bruce to join in.

Christmas came, and Bruce's birthday on the 26th. As usual, his aura took over the house. This was an especially big year because in February Bruce would be on his way to Parris Island for Marine Corps basic training. The countdown had begun, this time for real. He would be physically leaving the city, county, and state.

I wanted this time to pass as quickly as possible, more and more restless the longer he lived there. I was always worried I might come home and he wouldn't be at GED class, or everyone would be gone except us two. I could not wait for February to come and felt more on edge as the days passed. At times, I could feel my skin crawl.

Finally, the day arrived. My dad would be taking Bruce to the bus station, where he would meet other recruits to take the long bus ride to Parris Island, South Carolina—the East Coast Marines basic training facility. Bruce was packed up to go, with one small bag and a bunch of books to read on the way.

After all the goodbyes, my mom turned to me and said, "Why don't you give your brother a hug goodbye?"

I froze. I always wondered if Bruce saw me freeze, as he was only two feet away. "Um, what?" I let stumble out of my mouth.

"Why don't you give Bruce a hug before he goes?"

I did not know what to do. I turned and looked at Bruce. I wanted to vomit on him. He just blankly stared at me.

I could not believe what was being asked of me. I had not looked at Bruce's face since he abused me. But I couldn't make a scene because questions would be asked.

Also, Bruce was an inch away from being out of the house and free from the threat of prison. What might he had done to me, if I took that away from him right then and there? I was literally the only person standing between freedom and jail. I took the best option, him leaving.

The dynamic between us was weird, like both of us had

drawn pistols and were just waiting for the next move. Me, wondering if he would kill me to keep his secret, him probably wondering if I would tell someone and ruin his escape plan.

I leaned over and gave Bruce a halfhearted hug—and all at once, the shame, fear, and guilt all came back in a huge wave. I was disgusted with myself.

When Bruce left I went into my room and crawled into bed. I felt dreadful, to my bones, but he was gone. That was the only saving grace.

When I heard two car doors close, and the engine turned over, my problems were over. The idea that with the finality of a situation, its repercussions end—that was the foundation I was working from. *He's gone and I am safe and secure. Nothing can hurt me now.*

Except...except maybe myself.

The only thing I had to worry about now was Japan. The Japanese had consumed me, I was their prisoner. Japan was bringing truth and justice to my door.

The second half of fifth grade was our chapter on Japan, Land of the Rising Sun. That title must give shivers to many a Solace alum. We had to do a project for it and I did a big rice paddy, with papier-mâché for the rice fields and pine needles painted yellow for the rice. By the time I was done that project must have weighed about fifteen pounds—but I was done and it was a good project. After about three weeks of the class smelling of flour, I brought the project home on the bus and dumped it in the trash.

CHAPTER 6

One night at dinner, my mom put her fork down and said that she and my dad were going to Bruce's Marine Corps graduation in Parris Island. I nodded my head and kept on eating. She then said that I would be going with them, and my brother would be staying at my grandmother's house. Neither my brother nor I were happy about this situation whatsoever—my brother because my grandmother sucked, and me for obvious reasons.

My sister was staying home and not giving a fuck about that graduation. She was under no illusions that somehow the Marines could "cure" Bruce. Plus, she had not forgiven him for being a fucking terrorist who took my family hostage.

Pretty soon, Bruce was going to get an education on terrorism. It would come from a noise never heard on this planet before. During this time, a friend of my sister's, LT, came to live with us because her home life was untenable. Lose one, gain one. A much better one.

But that night at dinner, I really did not know how to react. I gulped so hard it hurt my throat, then just finished my meal in silence and excused myself to my room. I knew there was no way to talk my way out of it; I was going unless I wanted to confess about everything that had happened.

I had plenty of time to think about the whole ordeal I was in. It was so hard to wrap my head around what to do. I had no idea where I was going, or what my responsibilities were.

For the next couple nights, this whole process spun through my head. I didn't sleep much that week, or in the weeks to come. I felt like a caged animal who was about to be dragged through the dining room before they turned me into pâté. I did not want to make this trip, I was totally frightened and pissed, but I knew I had to make the best of it.

One thing is for sure, when I had walked through that intersection four years ago and made that decision, I meant it. No uncomfortable situation was going to change that. I never felt safe enough to tell anyone. My fight-or-flight was elevated, but that was my new normal, going forward.

I took a couple days' worth of schoolwork on the trip with me; my spring break was the week after. After the graduation we would be heading to my grandmother's house in Massachusetts. She wanted to see her newly minted Marine grandson.

We left on a Monday morning at the crack of dawn, drove most of the day, and ended up at a hotel in Roanoke, Virginia. Other than answering questions, I didn't speak pretty much the whole day. I just looked at the scenery and read.

When we got to the hotel, I quickly got changed and headed to the pool—a glorious sight for someone who's just finished a snowy Syracuse winter and rainy spring. Sometimes, it felt like I was drowning in mud. It felt at times that my world mirrored the outside weather.

We left early the next morning, drove for about an hour, and then stopped for breakfast. I was beginning to get restless. The closer we got to South Carolina, the queasier I got. I tried to do schoolwork and keep busy, but I was in a car going to a place I did not want to go, for a person who had hurt me to the core. My chest felt weird, tight and heavy—like someone was holding me down, sitting on my chest.

We got to our hotel, which was close to Parris Island, checked in and then went to the pool. I was the only one in the water and my parents were the only adults there. About an hour or two later, people started rolling in from all over the East Coast, for graduation. It was a party, for everyone except me.

The next day was Wednesday, and we could go to the base and meet Bruce. For all intents and purposes, his training was over. He would graduate from the Marine Corps in a few days. So, we packed up and headed to the base, on a long and lonely road. The only other ways off that island are through alligator-infested swamps, or the ocean.

I remember driving along and looking out at the swamp. The alligators sat on top of the water, just barely submerged, so they could soak up the warmth of the sun—and occasionally, I would see a pair of eyes, or a couple pairs, on the surface of the water. It had a very horror-film look to it: menacing eyes in the water, just staring at you; not knowing how long, or wide, these beasts were.

Since graduation was in a few days, there were parents walking with their sons all over the place. We found Bruce and my parents were ecstatic. He was alive, unhurt, and about to graduate. This graduation would expunge his police record and put all that behind him. Had he not graduated, he would have been returned to Syracuse to probably face arrest for assaulting the police officer.

Bruce the day before graduation. His bottom lip protruding with chew that my mother never noticed. In less than twenty-four hours, the United States Marine Corps will bless Bruce and his sins of the past will never be an impediment.

We walked along, and Bruce talked about his training: all the things he did, how he physically qualified, and his shooting classification. Basic training was still going on all around us. Parris Island produces about 17,000 recruits a year, and they do not stop for graduation.

As we walked, we came across a bunch of barracks, and walking by them, I noticed that the blinds on the windows were closed. Then, as we got closer, sets of eyes began to show in the windows—just like the gators, and just as creepy. Stephen King could not have come up with a scarier, more surreal moment. Bruce noted that these barracks held recruits that had failed basic training, for whatever reason, and had been charged with taking it over again, or being dismissed from the Corps.

On the other side of the barracks was a section of ground and a dozen or so of the redo recruits. They were on their hands, bodies horizontal in pushup position, legs running in place. As we walked by, one of the recruits looked up at us and his drill instructor was in his shadow in under a second. "Get your goddamn eyes on the ground. You do not deserve to look at those civilians. They are people and you are not."

Bruce just nodded.

As we kept walking the drill instructor looked up at us, saying, "Please do not make eye contact or comment to my recruits. They do not deserve your words or sympathies."

We walked around for a while more. It was like Parents' Day at summer camp: parents walking with their sons, taking pictures, exchanging stories, and getting to know each other again.

At the Post Exchange (PX), or bodega, we sat at a table, and my dad gave me five bucks to grab some food. I wandered around the huge cafeteria. Everywhere, parents sat with their sons, watching them eat and drink everything they had missed in the last thirteen weeks.

I ended up by a freezer, looking for something to help me beat the heat. I reached in and got a pint of Häagen Dazs chocolate. I got on line to pay and gave the woman the five-dollar bill when it was my turn. She reached in and gave me four ones and two quarters back. I looked at her quizzically and said, "Excuse me, you gave me back four dollars and fifty cents. I think that's a mistake."

She looked at me and said with a Southern accent, "Honey, that ice cream is only fifty cents."

I said thank you and walked over to the condiment stand, got a wooden spoon, and walked back to our table and sat down. It was a square four-person table, and my dad was on my right, Bruce on my left, and my mom across from me. I just sat there eating, in my own little world, head down and eyes on the table.

At one point, when my mom briefly left the table, my father reached across in front of me. I looked up and he was holding Bruce's lower lip. He pulled it out to expose a big brown line across his bottom set of teeth. "What is that?" my father asked.

"I don't smoke anymore," Bruce replied.

My dad let it go, saying, "Don't let your mother see that."

Bruce nodded. I don't know what was running through his mind, and didn't care, but he was acting like he was in the military, seemingly with more respect for my father—but brainwashing will do that to you. My parents didn't notice that I wasn't speaking to my brother, but that wasn't the kind of thing they would notice. They did not really care, they just wanted him to be a better person.

I did not care about anyone else's feelings about this event, my home life, or me. I was living my life by myself, having to make my best decisions for me. By this time my parents had thrown me the keys to my life and let me figure things out. That was just the way it was.

We hung out with Bruce for a while longer in the PX, exchanging stories about what he did in basic as I sat and ate my ice cream. After a while, we got up and wandered around the base a little more, watching different groups in different stages of the recruiting calendar come running by, chanting away. My dad and Bruce made plans for the next day and we said our goodbyes and headed for our hotel. I felt uncomfortable trying to sleep that night, which carried into the morning.

On the day of graduation, we woke up and got dressed. It was already 80 degrees by 6 a.m., but the humidity wasn't too bad yet. We headed toward Parris Island and stopped off at a diner that looked like a bomb had exploded, with dirty dishes on almost every table. We looked up and saw a waitress walking around furiously behind the counter, with an armful of plates. "Grab a seat at a clean table, if you can find one. I'll be right with you!"

We found a booth and took a seat. The waitress came wheeling by and we ordered. She was back in five minutes with our food and the check. We ate, my dad left some money on the table, and we headed off to graduation. Our car was already packed with our gear; we were heading right out after graduation to my grandmother's house in Massachusetts.

All I have to do is just close my eyes
To see the seagulls wheeling on those far distant skies
All I want to tell you, all I want to say
Is count me in on the journey
Don't expect me to stay.[4]

We got to the graduation: a very large parade ground with bleachers looking out, and no shade. When we sat down there was a single tall, black gentleman, standing all by himself in the middle of the parade ground, filling out about six-foot-three of a full Marine dress-blue uniform with saber. He looked as wide as he was tall. My mother asked my father about him and he gave a shrug.

My dad gave me his camera and I zoomed in on the man. He stood out there—face expressionless, dripping sweat, just waiting, at attention, until ten minutes before 9—then he snapped to attention and made his way off the tarmac. Parents and guests were in their seats and waiting.

Graduation started with music and marching. I was people-watching and checking out this very surreal place, about to watch my brother Bruce graduate from the United States Marine Corps, which was his penalty for punching a cop. He was not receiving any penalty for sexually assaulting me—because I told no one.

People made speeches, a whole lot of men with bright buttons and ribbons on their chests, and stars and piping on the shoulders of their drab-green dress uniforms.

Tree grove right off Parris Island parade ground. I was not happy.

As the ceremony moved along, we came to find out that the gentleman on the field before the ceremony had scored a perfect 300 on the United States Marine Corps Physical Fitness Test. The Marines had provided him with a full dress-blue uniform as reward for his hard work. Back then, it cost somewhere around $1,500 dollars, totally out of reach for a new recruit to afford. But this gentleman earned it the hard way. Now that Marine had to stand at full attention, so he could show everyone his new duds. Now that is some trolling by the United States Marines.

The recruits marched in, all sunburned with queer looks on their face; like they had just gotten laid, but couldn't tell anyone. (Keeping secrets, sound familiar?) There were more speeches and the band played some more. The men were proclaimed Marines and then asked to fall out—military for "You don't have to go home, but you got to get the fuck up out of here."

The new privates then threw their covers (hats, to civilians) into the air and cheered—then scrambled around like kids looking for them, because they had ignored their drill instructors' order to put something in their cover to identify it as theirs.

We eventually made our way out into the sea of people and found Bruce. He had a big grin on his face and my father and mother hugged him and were completely ecstatic. In a horrific replay of earlier events, my mother again told me to hug Bruce—now in public, for all to see, even if no one knew.

My dad was taking pictures, and eventually he got to me. I did not feel good about it at all. I knew close proximity to Bruce was coming, my anxiety was through the roof and I had to hold in every last bit of it. I was literally in mental jail: the mental fatigue bearing down on me, with no way to relieve it. I was exhausted and it was only 10:30 a.m.

I was forced to take a picture with Bruce and you can see in the picture, my hips are bent away from him. I did not want to be there, why would I? The whole event was a dance between Bruce, my parents, and me. *The United States government just told Bruce he's a great person and qualified to be in their Corps. Okay, we're leaving now.*

Finally, we got in the car and left. Bruce rode in the front seat with my dad and my mom rode in the back with me: a small miracle. We stopped at the first rest stop so Bruce could change. As Bruce walked out of the bathroom, an officer in uniform walked by, and Bruce almost knocked my mother over, snapping to attention. He'd gone from punching her out, fucked-up on drugs, to almost knocking her down while saluting an officer—all within a year and a half.

We got provisions and off we went, driving until late afternoon. I did homework and read, had conversations with my mom, but nothing I could concentrate on.

I remember my dad coming out with two keys when we checked into the hotel. He said that I would be rooming with Bruce because my parents had gotten their own room. I shrank to nothing in a second.

As we headed to the rooms I felt a tidal wave of anxiety, fear, and anger wash over me. But at the time, I had no name for these emotions and just thought they were my norm. I'd grown up with them. At times, now, it will appear that nothing bothers me—because my baseline of anxiety and fear is so much higher than your average human. But back then I was drowning in it, just hoping I would make it out alive.

We dropped our bags and went to dinner at some restaurant around the corner. I remember taking a long time to eat, trying to stretch out the time before I had to be alone with Bruce. Getting the check was like a sword swiping at my head.

When we got back to the hotel, I watched TV in my parents' room until it was time for bed. I was scared to go back to my room because my abuser was in there—but there was nothing I could do. Who could I tell? Who would believe me? Would I be signing my own death warrant by speaking out? I was scared, but I was also getting older, and wrestling with my freedom from Bruce. He was on a leash and I knew it.

Back in our room, I got ready for bed, taking the bed closest to the door. I climbed into bed; Bruce was watching something on TV. I just curled up and waited. He turned the light out and left the TV on. Eventually, I heard small snores from his side of the room. I didn't sleep one bit that night, gripping my blanket and sheet. *Wish I had my knife.*

I was up early. Bruce came out of the bathroom while I was zipping up my bag and tying my shoes. I went into the bathroom, and Bruce was already outside when I came out. They were packing up the car when I closed the hotel door behind me. I was exhausted and pretty much slept the whole way.

When we got to my grandmother's, she was ecstatic. Bruce was alive and looked good. He looked bigger—thirteen weeks of exercise will do that.

After hellos, and a big hug for me, my grandmother took my brother in the other room and talked to him. What about? I did not care. I imagine it was the same talk she gave her son, my mom's elder brother, who was fucking off while his father was in World War II. I am sure it was based on facts, love, and empathy. My uncle went on to become an engineer and not a criminal. Time will tell.

I went outside and wandered around. My grandparents' German shepherd, Baron, which my parents had given them, had been put to sleep, so there was no dog to follow me around the property. When Baron was alive and Rip was with us, the dogs would bark and jump and race up the stairs to meet us. Except this time no dog, and no Grandpa.

I missed him. I missed his slight whistle when he walked, and I missed watching him fiddle about. I was sure that he broke things just to fix them. I missed him making a fire if you mentioned you were cold, even in spring. I missed the smell of his pipe and him in his rocking chair, doing the crossword puzzle in pen. I missed what he was supposed to teach me. He and I were complete opposites, which I think was why I was so fascinated by him. He fiddled in the garage, did the crossword, read, watched *Meet the Press* on Sundays, and smoked Winstons. He loved his wife and family and his life was no more complicated than that.

In the side yard, behind the garage, were steps that led to the bottom backyard. A quick right and about fifty feet of stone wall led from my grandparents' yard to the half-acre of land my parents owned, which they ended up selling to a neighbor. We were going to build a house there, before Syracuse. *If only we had...* Maybe things would have been different.

But you cannot live in a world of maybes, so pondering such stupid questions is pointless. One thing I learned about from being abused: never think of the "what-ifs," because it can kill you. You have to think in the now, because if you don't, something will get past your guard and you'll be dead. Living in the world of what-ifs is akin to adhering to a religion. I have to live in the here and now, in the truth. I cannot live in a world of make-believe—it's too dangerous.

I made my way over to the frog pond, on the other side of the property. Fifty feet into the woods and there was the pond— the little frogs hopping around on the spring day. I went up on top of the large rock above the pond and gazed over my forest lands, watching the frogs go about their business.

Headed back to the house, instead of going inside I hopped up on top of the wall further down, which brought me to the back stairs, where Bruce threw up at my grandparent's fiftieth wedding anniversary, after he and my cousin D got wrecked.

I made my way up the stairs and across the wooden back porch. Here was where my mother heard my grandfather say "fuck" for the first time in her life, after she let go of a rope holding a jackhammer that accidentally smashed her father in his head.

I went in through the side door and closed it. My parents, Bruce, and my grandmother were all in the living room talking. I read a book while they chatted away.

For dinner, we would be going to my grandparents' favorite restaurant, Abraham Manchester's. It was originally a general store, but became a restaurant in the 1960s, and burned down in 2003.

We got dressed for dinner, Bruce wearing his new Marine service uniform, and off we went. At the restaurant, all eyes were on Bruce. My grandmother was on his arm and I was walking behind my parents. The people in the restaurant were looking and murmuring about my brother, the spectacle walking through the dining room.

As Bruce soaked up all the attention, I just sat, staring at the menu and wondering when it would stop. I had a cheeseburger and apple pie.

We headed home and changed. Since it was a cool night, my dad made a fire and a drink for him and my grandmother. They stayed up and chatted and I just sort of zoned out. The house was different without my grandfather and I did not like it. We all went to bed; I slept on the floor near the fireplace, like old times when we all visited.

But when I woke, my grandfather did not make his walk through the living room, to get the two glasses of orange juice for him and his missus. Things were not the same anymore. They never would be.

We got up and headed out for church with my grandmother, then headed back to her place for breakfast and to pack up. I took a quick walk around the yard, while my mother said her goodbyes. My grandmother hugged me, scrunched her nose, and smiled. "Alright dear," she said in her slight Jersey accent.

I got into the back seat and we headed out to the cemetery near the church, to pay our respects at my grandfather's gravesite. I hated being there. I felt I had not had enough time with this man.

Then it was back in the car, all four of us headed for home. Bruce would be staying with us for a couple days before he had to head to his new training in Fort Knox, Kentucky. It was a quiet ride home for me, in the back seat with my mom. I had made it all the way without having a breakdown. Looking back at that surreal moment, I feel as though I floated through that whole car ride. My defensive posture, from when Bruce lived at home, was automatic. I didn't understand it at the time, but the closer I got to home, the more I reverted to fear and defense.

I wondered what was going through Bruce's head. He never turned around, even when he was speaking with my mom. When he answered a question, Bruce would put the visor down and use the mirror. He had to know I was avoiding him, but I really did not care what he thought—if I was making him uncomfortable, great.

Bruce's MOS (Military Occupational Specialty) was 1812, Tank Crewmember. He would attend the Abrams M1A1 Armor Crewmember course and become qualified for a tanker position.

I laid as low as possible during those last days he was home. I had school, so I was gone during the day, then off to baseball practice or games. If neither was happening that day, I hung out with Dan or Garrett. I made sure to never be home alone with Bruce— I still did not feel safe with him in the house.

My anxiety shot up quite a bit with him home. I hadn't really given any thought to the prospect of him coming home with us, too caught up in dealing with just the graduation. I was angry with myself for not adding that variable into the equation. With Bruce home, I felt like a thin piece of plastic had been placed over my entire life. Everything I did became just a little bit harder. I had a new card thrown into my hand and I did not know how to play it. Something new—or actually something old —was in the background all the time now.

It took the wind out of me. I had felt so free to move around the house, the neighborhood—now here I was, back to being hypervigilant. I constantly had to figure out Bruce's next move, to keep myself safe. I was back to being fearful and scared all the time; emotions that I thought were gone were now back, more powerful than ever. I was back in emotional jail and the warden came home. Who knows if my parents could have kept me safe, but I was not taking chances.

We also had a new roommate—a friend of my sister's was having some static at home and had come to live with us. She was nice and I liked her very much, but I wanted some room for me, a little space to breathe.

Bruce left for Fort Knox at the end of the week. No hug goodbye this time. I was happy to be safe again.

Around this time, my parents received a letter from the Syracuse Board of Education. My sister, who is extremely bright, and had been getting pretty much straight As, was not going to graduate on time. She had been about to finish high school, but there was a kink thrown into the process: gym class, which she had been skipping, to go to the library and study. The state required that you attend a minimum number of gym classes per year to satisfy your graduation requirements. My sister was about to fail her senior year in high school.

My dad and mom were both hopping fucking mad. My sister was failing to realize that there was not some kind of quick fix. They were pissed because she had come this far and worked so hard, and it all was about to be ruined. My sister was going to have to make up her gym class during the next fall semester, would not be graduating on time, and everyone was pissed.

Truthfully, she is the only one that should have been pissed, but to this day the subject still pisses off my dad, which is why I try to bring it up as often as I can. It's fun!

CHAPTER 7

Back at home, summer started, and I spent a lot of time hanging around the neighborhood. During the day, if Dan and Garrett were busy, I would ride my bike over to Barry Park. It was new for me, riding out of the neighborhood and seeing new things; up to this point, I only saw other neighborhoods from the inside of a car. Now, I was rolling through and checking things out for myself, going down streets I had never been down, at my own speed.

At the park, I didn't know anyone. My school was in the other direction, and no one from Solace ever came there to play. But I just went in blind, and it was fun. They had one of the old-school horizontal spinning wheels (the Wheel of Death), with the metal piping interior to hang on to—a big one that could probably fit ten or twelve kids on it. I would spend a couple hours there and ride around the running paths across the street at the pond.

Barry Park was a good new adventure for me. I honestly do not remember anyone's name that I met there. Two close friends who I would meet years later lived in the neighborhood at the time, plus a bunch of people I would meet over the next couple years lived around the park. I probably ran across them without even knowing.

At night we played either kick-the-can or manhunt. It was great, running around the neighborhood and playing games with the locals. Some of the kids from Seeley, a neighborhood around the corner from Solace, came over and played with us.

Good weather meant that my family would eat outside, over at my grandmother's house. I was already there once a week mowing the lawn. My father was happy to bequeath the chore to me; once I was mobile on the bike *(shit)* I was able to come over and mow the grass and listen to her degrade my family and cousins.

I did not mind going to her house for dinner, most of the time. My grandmother's friends were all retired nurses and were way fucking cooler than she was. They were funny and inquisitive, and always had a good story that bordered on being a little sketchy, ethically or legally at times. They all belong to a card club called the Corinthian Club that was in an old mansion.

One night, three of her friends were also over for dinner, still in their Sunday best. My parents and a priest from Our Lady of Solace were outside cooking on the grill and chatting. I was inside with my grandmother's three friends, playing rummy. My brother and sister were not much for cards, plus they were outside putting in their time so they could leave right after dinner.

We paired up, and my partner was one of my grandmother's friends who I really liked. She was married to a farmer, lived south of the city in Tully, and had no children. Her stories were always fun.

We were playing a hand and my partner made a comment to the woman on my left, her right. The other woman looked over at my partner and they had a quick, hard laugh. They both looked over at the third woman, and now all three were laughing. So, my partner started to relay the story to all of us.

All three ladies had been working in the same hospital when there was an emergency: a very bad mining or construction accident with some fatalities and many injuries. They went to help with the overflow, which spilled out of the emergency room and down the hall, gurneys on either side of the hallway. At one point, they realized that some of the rock debris had exposed rock salt, common in the area. Men were screaming at the top of their lungs, not only from the rock shrapnel, but from the literal salt in their wounds.

As she told the story, the other women chimed in with rejoinders and quips of their own, spicing up the story and jogging memories. They were sitting there chuckling, sipping their Manhattan drinks and tossing cards.

Then my partner settled down and said, "We had to take action." She said that she met with the other two ladies to come up with a plan. The emergency room was overflowing and doctors and nurses alike could not hear themselves think. It was becoming dangerous.

So, the ladies marched down to the medication cage and keyed in. They took out boxes of syringes and whatever opioid was on hand. They started to draw syringes in three doses, according to body size—small, medium, and large—then proceeded to walk down the hallway and inject each patient. They waited to see if there was any immediate reaction, and then finished emptying the syringe into each man, making sure not to give too much and pulling back as soon as someone showed relief. Soon the hallway was relatively silent compared to the previous chaos.

The ladies kept playing, sipping their drinks, and laughing the whole time this story was told. I was in shock! They were so fucking gangster and they didn't even know it.

The summer was coming to a close. My mom and dad had been tense the whole summer. Once the Marines got involved in Beirut, their moods took on new levels of worry. By this time, Bruce had graduated from tanker school as a loader and got sent to Camp Lejeune, North Carolina, to the 24th MAU. It was the very same base as the Marines currently in Beirut.

Back home, I had plenty to do and was sleeping better, comparatively, since I was getting a lot of exercise. I hated my school and was beginning to question everything about the Catholic church. Garrett and Dan were the only reason it was bearable.

I still had my morning paper route, so when school started up again I was up early as usual and out the door. We had a new sixth-grade teacher. I was still the class clown and the new teacher was not a fan. I could sympathize with him—I wasn't a fan of me either. I was still running on a bunch of anger, witticisms aside, which I expressed in the classroom whether people wanted to hear it or not.

My brother had started his sophomore year at his high school. My sister was finishing up her last half-year of high school, and her friend, LT, was still living with us. I liked LT a lot. She was nice and funny, and I think my sister needed her after the last couple of years. My sister lost her "big sister" when my cousin C moved out, and now she had a new "sister" her own age.

Having more girl energy around softened my dad up a bit. The only women in my dad's life until he had gotten married and had children were his grandmother, his mother, and then my mom. He didn't hang out with girls much, growing up. In the 1940s and '50s, society still kept the sexes from intermingling as much as possible.

So, my dad hadn't hung out with girls like I did as I grew up. The girls in my neighborhood played stickball or manhunt or kick the can, like anyone else. We all played in the same baseball league in Salt Springs.

Women provide a softening to the world but are not, for the most part, allowed to talk about it. In all the years I knew my grandmother, I never heard her say "I love you" to him—or anyone. His grandmother died before she could provide him with enough love.

My sister and LT would push my dad to the limit: blasting music, slamming things, and just being loud in general. There were now two high school women in the house, and my father was about to get an education. The B52's, Elvis Costello, and the Ramones were my father's "who the hell is that" moment as a parent. They were happy to tell him.

I, on the other hand, started school at Our Lady of Solace. Dan's older sister had gone on to high school to be with the cool kids, so now it was us and Dan's little sister walking to school. We would walk the same route to school we did every day, right across my Rubicon. Sixth grade started much like fifth: newspapers, school, home for a quick change and some food; then tackle football down at the church, and then back home. But, no chaos.

I was late to after-school fun about one day a week on average, hit with a lot of detention, either by my teacher, Mr. K, or the seventh-grade teacher, Mr. F. I am sure I am responsible for removing some years from those men's lives. I was always quick with a remark or a joke, which often went just a little too far. I don't know how much detention my parents knew about, probably not much because they never said anything.

One of the only good things about being an altar boy is getting out of school sometimes; the sad part is that it's for funerals. Every once in a while, you get a call and you get out of class. My first time that year came that fall. I went over with my partner and got everything all set up. I remember being up on the altar and looking out on the crowd, and I actually saw someone I knew: my grandmother.

As the ceremony went along, I tried my best to spot who was in the casket. When I finally got a chance, I craned my neck to see who it was. It was one of my grandmother's friends who I had met once or twice before. I had seen her around the church, but never spoke to her other than to say hello to her at the church and at my grandmother's house. Nearly everyone in the church was crying, or at least very upset, except my grandmother, who was dry-eyed and just kind of watching. I did not expect much from her, emotionally, but this was more than I could understand.

The fall went along: warm days, cold nights, and the slow, steady drop of a few degrees in temperature a day. And then you wake up one day at the end of October and it is cold as fuck out, and that is your winter wake-up call. The next one will be snow. I was getting to know my sixth-grade teacher well with my frequent detentions.

Christmas was fast approaching and it felt different this year, a lot less tension and anxiety. The last four Christmases had just sucked: Bruce's behavior and actions in- and outside the house overshadowed any sense of fun for the day.

But even though things had lightened up in the house immensely, I still felt this slight, gnawing bit of anxiety: another layer between me and the world. Things got tougher, but I couldn't understand why.

Once Bruce was out of the house, my sister moved down to the other side of the dining room table, across from me. LT now sat next to my mom, across from my brother. Dinner with my sister and I can be an animated affair, to say the least: lots of references to *Three Stooges* (whom my father abhors) and *It's a Wonderful Life.* My father would go a little nutty from all of our laughter. Also, my sister had a habit of showing her ABC (already been chewed) food to my dad. He would be eating quietly, lost in thought; my sister would open her mouth and stare at him until he looked up. Invariably this would get an "Oh Jesus" from my dad and a "What, what is it?" from my mom. I would start to laugh and my sister's belly would jiggle while she ate.

As I was very susceptible to peer pressure and fun, and now that Bruce was gone, of course I joined in with the food shenanigans. This did not bring any kind of delight to my father at all. The barrage of ABC food and my sister's comments on the contents of his plate brought a new witticism to the table. She took great pride in twisting my dad and having fun with him. I'm pretty sure no one had ever interacted with my dad that way, and to a degree it loosened him up. To this day my sister and I are not allowed to eat next to each other in my dad's presence.

Christmas came and went and I don't remember if Bruce called. If he did I'm sure I was somewhere else. Anytime he called home, I would do anything to extricate myself from having to talk to him. I would go to my room, shovel the snow, walk the dog, whatever it took.

At the beginning of February, I got called to be an altar boy at another funeral across the street. I went across and ran through the service: no grandmother this time, or anyone I knew. I finished up and went back across the street to school.

I looked around to see what people were doing and it did not look familiar to me, so I walked up to the teacher's desk to get the work, and sat down. After looking it over real quick, I got started and then raised my hand. I asked a question that apparently had been addressed at the beginning of class, which I was not there for. I made a remark that my teacher did not care for and then he made a remark back to me, which brought everyone's pencils down.

I then got my "Why don't you go fuck yourself" look on my face, which did not incur his wrath as much as the middle finger coming from my arm, bent at a 90-degree angle on my desk.

Once he looked up and saw that finger, he was up and out of his seat in a hurry. He was about six-foot-four and those legs made some quick-ass strides to me. I had my finger up still— I really should have put it down. The next thing I knew I was standing upright, with my arm in the air and his hand around my wrist. "To the office, now!!" he said in a positive, loving and sympathetic voice.

I sat down outside the principal's office, having been through the routine once or twice already and seen other cellmates run the gauntlet. My teacher went inside the office and closed the door.

After about two minutes he emerged and went back to class. Sister Patrick (HNIC—Head Nun in Charge) came to the door frame and nodded me in. To be fair, she was not as angry as I thought she should be. She just gave me the general riot act and stated how I was probably just having a bad day and the funeral didn't help. Since I had my books, she had me read outside her office until the bell and I went back to home class. The day went on and I just went home after school as usual.

After dinner, my parents called me into the kitchen. *Jig's up.* My mom had just gotten off the phone with Sister Patrick and was told what had transpired in the classroom. My parents asked me for my side of the story, and I provided absolutely no exculpatory evidence for my own defense. I talked to my parents about my general dislike for the school. None of my siblings were in private school any longer and I was wondering why I still was. After some debate, and apparently a request that I not come back to Solace next year, it was decided I would go to public middle school.

So that is my secret formula for not going to Catholic school any more, for just $19.95*!! Shipping and handling not included. *Must provide own middle finger.

I was pretty damn excited when my parents told me I would be going to a different school. I was sick of the whole Catholic school nonsense, and I was becoming more disillusioned with religion every day. It took a couple of days to sink in that I would be leaving Garrett and Dan for the first time. They had been by my side since kindergarten, and I was having a very eerie feeling about leaving them. That was the one drawback, our separation.

The school year carried on with me and the teachers in an informal truce. I lightened up a bit, knowing I was not coming back. I am sure they were happy not to have me.

Bruce was done with tank school and all of its endeavors and was stationed at Camp Lejeune, North Carolina, training and getting ready for his first assignment. He sent a letter around March or April, filling my parents in and stating that he was in tank school, soon to graduate. Then he went quiet. My parents were told through a letter from Bruce that he had been ordered to a tank of his own, as a loader in the 24th Marine Amphibious Unit or, 24th MAU.

My father knew that there was a rotation coming for the Middle East; it was in the newspapers and on the news. 1,200 United States Service Members were stationed in Beirut, Lebanon after Israel had invaded the year before. Buildings were being blown up and people were dying. The new replacements for Beirut would be coming from Camp Lejeune, North Carolina, my brother's new post.

The following are headlines and excerpts of newspaper articles that my parents would be bombarded with about the escalation of violence on a nightly basis. Along with the news, in 1982 there was no twenty-four-hour news cycle. The person who would bring home Beirut's death and destruction for my parents was me, the newspaper delivery boy.

They were reading these stories every night. The more they read, the more troubling it was. They didn't tell me how they felt, and I didn't care to ask.

I walk forty-seven miles of barbed wire
I use a cobra snake for a necktie
I got a brand new house on the roadside
Made from rattlesnake hide.[5]

May 30 and 31
Guerrillas ambush Israelis, kill 2, wound 3
Syria warns of possible U.S. casualties
Israel sustains another ambush with fatalities and wounded. Israel is attacked daily, all over Lebanon, by both military and asymmetrical combatants. Syria threatens that new war in Lebanon with Israel could possibly result in U.S. casualties.

Neither article mentioned the changing from the 32nd MAU to the 24th MAU.

Bruce was now in Beirut. The anxiety level reached a whole new level, for my parent's and by extension, me. 1,200 other US soldiers' families too. While the rest of America was going out to eat, getting drinks, going clubbing, reading books, watching shows, and going about their daily lives, a certain segment of the population was living and breathing on a daily basis by the word of the president, the secretary of defense, and the national news reporter at 6 p.m. EST.

It was my last couple of weeks at Solace forever. It did not really hit me until the last week that I would be without Garrett and Dan the following year. It was a daunting thought and I would not know how hard it would be until later.

April 19

Embassy toll at 24; 23 presumed dead
On April 18, a suicide driver using a van stolen from the embassy the year before, full of an estimated 2,000 pounds of explosives, rammed through the security gate and straight through to the United States embassy lobby, where it exploded. Sixty-one people were killed; seventeen were Americans. Of the seventeen Americans killed, seven were CIA employees, including Chief of Station (COS) Ken Hass, his deputy James Lewis, and his wife, who started work that morning. Also killed in the blast was Robert C. Ames, CIA national intelligence officer for the Near East, who happened to be visiting. That was a major hit to our spying capabilities, with soldiers on the ground just a few miles away. Hass was replaced by new station chief, William Buckley.

June 1
Syria: U.S. Blood Will Flow in War
Syria warns U.S. to call off Israel, or Marine blood will flow. Both Syria and Israel are building up troops along their cease-fire lines. Israeli jets fly reconnaissance flights and no shots fired upon. Israeli positions were shelled during cease-fire, but did not return fire.

June 2
Khadafy Urges War on Israel
Khadafy (Muammar) calls on Arab world and youth to wage war against the U.S.

June 4
Israeli Broadcast Says Haig Gave Tacit Approval for Lebanon Raid
Israeli radio states Alexander Haig, then Secretary of Defense, gave tacit approval of Lebanon invasion by Israel the summer before.

June 6
War in Lebanon Hurts Israel

My mom and dad watched and read anything they could get their hands on regarding Beirut. Their stress was obvious and at times they seemed a little aloof, thinking about Bruce. There was political posturing not only from our government, but also from the other governments and warlords involved in the conflict. Bullets were flying and people were talking shit. That is very dangerous, and to parents and loved ones who knew soldiers there, it was nerve-racking.

June 11
Bomb Misses Israeli Convoy
6 Lebanese Injured, Marine Compound Rattled

Back in Syracuse, school was finally over, and off I went. If there was a fuck to be given that day, you would not find it sowing in my field. I was done with Solace, and it was done with me. I was no longer an altar boy, so that was off my plate on Sunday mornings as well. Kinda.

June 18
Israeli Siege Draws Moslem Revenge Vow

July 1
Israel Rejects New Pullout Plan

July 3
Shultz Sent Back on Mideast Mission
30,000 Will Not Leave, PLO Escalates Fight

CHAPTER 8

We went to my grandmother's house for the Fourth of July as usual. My sister poked her head in—she had moved into an apartment near the Salt City Theater. A friend of the family, MK, was at my grandmother's, along with the priest who worked at Solace church, TK, and his sister Joan. I played cards with Joan as usual.

I remember sitting in the backyard as the adults discussed Bruce and the situation in Beirut. Ever more, my parents' anxiety was increasing, making them short-tempered, confused, not totally paying attention to what was going on. My parents' disinterest in my life increased.

It was weird having my parents' focus be so intensely on Bruce, despite how horrible his behavior was, but I had never made it clear to anyone what happened. I kept it all a secret, but I was enraged no one was coming to help. It is a conundrum that, when I look back on, I can only shake my head at. Screaming in a silent rage at the secrets that I kept, and knowing no one would save me as a result.

My parents never really asked me anything other than "How was your day?" and "Can you mow the lawn?" But life was so shitty in so many other ways, it did not register as unfair at the time; I didn't know what I was missing. When you grow up not getting enough oxygen, you get used to your blue skin.

July 10
Syria Warns Against Aggression, Says It's Ready to Talk
Israel Talks Redeployment

July 11
Israelis Begin 'Trial' Pullback
Troops Leave Beirut Hill Positions; West Bank Bolstered

July 15
Gunfire Rocks Beirut
LAF and Muslim militias fought with machine guns and grenades in downtown Beirut. LAF attempted to evict Shiite squatters from a school. Three LAF wounded, one militia killed, three wounded.

July 19
Gemayel Meets Hussein
On the way to US to ask for more money and troops, Amin Gamayel stops in France to talk to King Hussein of Jordan. PLO split is encouraging. Neither Hussein nor Gemayel made any substantive comments.

The summer went along as previous summers had, but people were changing. This would be the last summer of kick the can and manhunt, as the majority of the kids were moving into high school. Drugs, booze, and sex—you know, fun!—were taking their place. Dan and I were heading into seventh grade, and we would start doing different things at night. It was still a fun summer, hanging out with Dan and Garrett during the day and running around at night. I had a freedom that I'd never really had before—not only getting older, but with Bruce gone. I felt a little better, even though the stew was still cooking on the back burner of my mind.

July 20
Israel to Pull Back Troops in Lebanon; Seven-Year-Old Girl Killed

July 21
Gemayel Opposes Partial Troop Withdrawal

President Amin Gemayel insists Israel fully withdraw instead of partial, insists it would split country. Israel wants to pull back just 11 miles south of Beirut for better defensive positions.

Israel to Channel Weapons to Nicaragua
Action Comes at U.S. Request; Supply Route to Be Via Honduras
Israel is "urged" by Reagan administration to send weapons taken from PLO soldiers and send them to Honduras, which will then send them to Nicaragua to help supply the right wing rebel group known as the Contras.

July 22
Beirut Airport Shelled; One Killed
Us Marine, Navy Air Controller Among 12 Injured in Attack

July 25
Us, Israel to Huddle; Lebanon Fights Mount

August 4
Talk with Begin Encourages McFarlane
Israelis Offer "Constructive' Views on Lebanon Troop Withdrawal
Special Envoy Robert McFarlane, appointed last week after Syrians denounced Special Envoy Philip Habib as too pro-Israel. McFarlane states that he has seen a "promise of progress" to get troops out of Lebanon. Israeli troops are pulling out of mountain positions just north of the city of Sidon.

August 11
Druze vow to Continue Shelling Until Government Resigns

Somewhere around this time, we got a letter from Bruce explaining the situation on the ground and day-to-day living. The Amal and Shiite militia in the hills open fire with artillery for about twenty or thirty minutes. The Marines send a message up the chain of command to shoot back, but by the time the message was received the militia were packed up and moved on down the road.

Bruce wrote about the frustration of random mortars, shells, and bullets that made it into the Marine compound. My parents send him a huge box of books he had requested.

August 14
Lebanese Envoy Asks for More Troops
US Help Sought to Avoid 'Death And Destruction' as Israelis Pull Back
Militias' Battle in Lebanon

August 16
Beirut Airport Reopens; Marines to Shoot Back
Demand that Christians stay out of Muslim strongholds in the mountains overlooking the airport.

August 17
Fear Mounts for Safety of Palestinians

As we neared the first week of school, my anxiety grew. It would be my first time going to school—a new school—without Dan and Garrett there. I'd be walking to school with a kid I knew from baseball, and also kind of knew this one girl who was friends with one of my classmates at Solace, but none of this was doing me any good. Walking a new route, to a new place, and meeting a bunch of new people brought on a new anxiety. A new layer wrapped around me. It got harder to stay in conversations. I wanted to talk less about me and my home, changing the subject when those topics came up. Everything I did got a little harder as my mind wandered, wondering if I was safe and secure.

Just before school started, my parents were out one night and the phone rang. I answered and a gentleman introduced himself, wanting to speak to my dad. I told him he was out and offered to take a message. He stated that he was with the AP and that he had pictures of Bruce. I took a message and when my dad came home, I told him of the call. He put his thumb on his index and middle finger and rubbed them, indicating money, but I shook my head no. The gentleman had not mentioned money for these pictures. It was late, so my dad took the number.

This man had pictures of Bruce, in Beirut, and the pictures were about to be printed in newspapers all over the country. My abuser was about to become famous.

August 25
Blast Rips through Building Holding French Peacekeepers Killing at Least 2 and Wounding 3

August 27
More Marines May Be Sent to Lebanon

August 29
Marines on Attack
Offensive Follows Shelling Fatal to 2

August 30
Shots Hit French
One Killed in Beirut; British Under Fire
Begin Is Firm on His Resignation
Begin stands firm on resignation. Resignation does not become official until he hands written statement to state president. Friends are convinced he will go through with this.

August 31
Lebanon Sends 10,000 Troops against Druze, Shiite Militias

September 1
Fighting in Lebanon Eases as Army Mops Up
Funeral Tuesday for Slain Marine
Parents of slain Marine from Henrietta [suburb of Rochester and west of Syracuse] will travel to Pennsylvania to attend their son's funeral. Eric Hammel's book *The Root* makes reference to Staff Sergeant Ortega's death and burial.

Shultz Doubts Marines Are Targets
Conflicting Messages Intercepted in Beirut
Lebanese Muslims Shell US Ambassador's House

September 2
2,000 Marines Ordered to Stand By off Beirut
Reagan cuts short 25-day vacation and sends 2,000 more Marines to sit off Lebanon coast. Reagan receives criticism for riding horse and doing chores instead of being in Washington.

September 3
Marines Eulogize Dead
Buddies Join in Tribute to 2 Killed in Beirut

September 4
Israelis Begin Pullout
Rival Militias Clash in Peaks Near Beirut

September 6
Beirut Rocket Attack Kills 2 Marines
September 6 was the first day of school at Aaron T. Levy Magnet Middle School, and I was shitting a brick. Luckily, my paper route gave me a good long time to dwell on my new adventure. I met a kid and his sister I knew and we walked up East Genesee Street, toward downtown.

The school was seventh and eighth grades and was split into two teams for each grade: seventh grade was teams 1 and 2 and eight grade was teams 3 and 4, about 125 people each. This grouping established who your teachers were, when you ate lunch, etc. I was team 2. Go team 2!

I remember getting to school, and the kid's sister left to go be with her friends, and I hung out with a few friends of the kid until the bell. I distinctly remember the mental gulp I took then. It hurt.

I went to my homeroom and walked in. I said hello to my teacher and did not even notice anyone else in class. My eyes were glued to the ground and I was afraid to look up. I felt naked without Garrett and Dan—no one to lean on or talk to. A familiar voice or laugh would have put me at ease. I had neither.

When I looked up after sitting down, I saw a few kids across the room. There were a couple of Asian kids in the first row, quietly talking and joking to themselves in their native tongue. I just sat there eating my anxiety for second breakfast and truly disliking the taste. After a few more minutes, some more Asian kids came in and joined the first group, or sat in a separate group. After a few more minutes, a pale white kid with a mop of curly, sandy-blond hair and a very striped shirt came in and sat to my left. He did the same thing I did, walking in with head down, and it was not until he looked up that he realized he was sitting next to someone. He said good morning. His name was PS and he was my first friend in my new school, and I still know him today. He still has the curly, sandy hair, but has pulled back on the stripes thankfully.

The bell rang, and the teacher came out from behind her desk, introduced herself, and started to take attendance. She asked us each to introduce ourselves and say where we were from. She started calling names, butchering each and every one of the Asian kids' names but taking each correction cheerfully. Our school was a magnet school that bused in kids from outside the district, so we had kids from everywhere: Vietnam, Thailand, Dominican Republic, Puerto Rico, Russia, Germany, Poland, and several countries in the Middle East, to name a few. We probably had at least fifteen nationalities and six or more religions.

The first couple days of school were rough. I kept my eyes

down and just tried to watch. Humor was the only thing I had going for me so I just looked for my moments to say something funny, to try and endear some people to me. I had never really had to go out and make new friends before. They came prebaked every September at Our Lady of Solace. And with just two grades, there were a limited amount of people I could meet.

It was overwhelming, walking down the hall not knowing anyone. I was not the best-dressed in class, or wearing a fancy new backpack or new school clothes, so my self-esteem was already a little shot. Plus, whatever confidence I'd had was blown to bits that day in Bruce's room. Four years later and Bruce was still winning.

September 7
Syracuse Marine Wounded in Beirut
One of the Marines injured was from Eastwood, not ten minutes from my house. The mother spoke of a letter she received from her son before they started being shelled, where he talked about Israeli bombings and the crying and screams they heard. All they could do is watch it on the news.

3 French Soldiers Killed
Lebanon: How Can Shultz Say We Aren't in "Hostilities"?

September 8
Navy Joins Beirut Fray
Ship, Marines Return Druze Artillery Fire

September 9
Marines Unharmed in Rocket Barrage

September 10
50 Lebanese Civilians Massacred As Cease-Fire Fails
Rightists Claim 110 Christians Killed by Druze Muslims in Mountains; Iranian Gunmen Reported on Way to Beirut

September 12

Marines Return Fire
3 Companies Engage Militia; No Yanks Hurt

September 13
Reagan Approves Use of Airstrikes

September 14
Reagan Action Hints Bigger Role in Lebanon
Lebanese Army Claims It Halted Druze Attack
LAF Prevented Druze from Another Attack on Souk El-Gharb

September 15
War Jets Warn Druze; Israeli Soldier Killed

September 16
Lebanon Loses One-Fifth of Tiny Air Force
1 Plane Shot Down, 2 Hit; Druze Shell Marine Base

September 17
Arafat Returns as Lebanese Attack

September 18
US Navy Pounds Druze Near Beirut
New UN Force Proposed to Keep Peace in Lebanon
All 3 British Carriers Sail to Mediterranean

My life had become routine, I needed it to be. Wake up and deliver papers, go to school, then tackle football down at the church if it did not rain. Once home, eat dinner, do homework and then watch TV. Garrett was also at a new school, Christian Brother's Academy (CBA). I think he was just as bummed having to leave me and Dan as I was leaving him and Dan. I knew one thing: he did not like his new school at all. This was the first routine of my choosing ever.

September 20

French, US Jets Airborne over Lebanon

September 21
Fighting Intensifies in Lebanon
Druze artillery and tanks pound Souk-el Gharb.
(Picture) A Marine lying down, behind some sandbags, reading a book. It's Bruce, the picture the guy was referring to in the phone call. Listed his full name, that he graduated from Nottingham (really?), plus a quote from my dad and our address. It was a surreal thing to see Bruce in Beirut, just reading. The action does not match the news headlines.

September 22
Lebanese Stop Druze Attack
Lebanon: We're Getting in Deeper Without Knowing Why
OP-ED Fire responses can now be afforded to MNF (Multi National Force) troops if they are fired upon. Any threat to any MNF can now expect a US response.

September 23
Mideast Truce Hopes Brighten

September 24
Beirut Fighting Fiercer; USS New Jersey Added

September 25
US Battleship Arrives to Help Defend Lebanon

September 27
Lebanese Prime Minister Resigns; Truce Off to Shaky Start
The morning paper that my dad bought had the second picture of Bruce, squatting on the front corner of his Abrams tank, barefoot, sticking a big-ass chew in his mouth. My mother now knows her son chews. She was not happy.

Truce holds despite sniping
Despite a truce being negotiated, snipers were shooting at Marine positions.

September 28
Army, Militias Attempt to Save Lebanese Truce

September 29
American Soldiers Abducted in Beirut, Freed by Militia

September 30
Lebanon Optimistic Despite Truce Violations

October 2
Eight Local Marines Get Taste of Warfare
Tapes and Letters Home Reflect Concern about US Involvement, Beirut Poverty
Relatives of the eight Marines were interviewed for a local article. My dad was quoted. This was a hard read for me.

Bruce squatting on his M1 Abrams battle tank. My mother noticed the pouch of chew, my father noticed he was barefoot. This picture and article would draw major attention to me at school, but not in a positive way. Just that people knew who I was.

Rights attained from Getty Images

It was not lost on your average reader that this event in Beirut was enormously powerful and dangerous. Marines were dying, civilians were dying, and my parents were on a razor's edge. I could only think about what all those other parents and relatives must have been going through. My parents read the newspaper and so did they. They must have been as much on edge as my parents were.

This is the side the general public never sees when they know of deployed troops: the people left behind left to worry and wonder. The average citizen does not care about the deployed troop because they have no skin in the game. Reprint of the bare-foot tank picture of Bruce. Upsets mother more that son is seen by millions with a big-ass chew.

October 3
Druze Leader Forms Rebel Government

One evening, I had just gotten done playing football at the church and was walking home when I noticed a TV van in front of my house. What fun!!

As I approached, I could see my mom and dad being interviewed by one of the local TV stations. The pictures of Bruce had brought more media attention.

I walked across the driveway to the front yard, my mom said hello, and I waved at my dad, who was in between takes. A couple feet away from the front step, I felt someone behind me.

As I neared the front door, I turned around. It was the TV production assistant, close on my trail. "Hey. Hey, excuse me. How would you like to be on TV?"

"No, thank you," I said, dumbfounded as to why I was acting polite. Was I growing up?

"I was just thinking you might want to," he persisted.

I gave the man a look that stopped him in his tracks. I was tempted to open the front screen and let Rip out. He was on a downward slope with hip-dysplasia, but the sound of his bark and the sight of him could still make bitches shit themselves. But my parents would have been angry at me for almost killing the media. I just shrugged the guy off and went inside. My parents were going to be on TV in about ten minutes. I just wanted all this media and attention to be gone. All of this attention was invading my space, which was already spilling over with parental anxiety due to Bruce being in a war zone.

I wanted all of it to be over with. I did not really care about Bruce being in Beirut one way or another. What I did not like was what it did to my parents. They were the ones who were living on the daily news, hoping that it would not report Bruce's death before the government did. All parents go through that when their child is in a war zone. It creates a bubble of fear and anxiety. My subconscious did not differentiate the difference between their anxiety and mine, so it just followed along. It was surreal feeling that Bruce was famous, despite what he did to me.

October 5
Diplomats Fearful of War Escalation as 6 Die in Fighting

October 6
Lebanese Peace Talks Appear One Step Closer

October 7
Lebanese: Muslims Battle

October 9
Marine from Minoa Is Serving in Beirut
Syria Has New Missiles from Russia: Reagan

October 10
Paul Cooper's Sending Sweet Memories of Home to Our Marines in Lebanon

October 11
Damper on Peace Talks

October 14
Marine Killed by Sniper Fire
Another Is Hurt Near Beirut Slum

October 16
Shooting Back, Marines Kill 4

October 17
National Security Choice: McFarlane
Sniper Hideouts Shelled in Lebanon

October 18
Lebanon Talks Start Thursday
Gunmen Who Killed Marines Withdraw from Shiite District

October 19
Car Bomb Injures 2 Marines
Slain Marine Praised As Hero

October 20
Lebanese Leaders Asked to Confer in Switzerland

October 21
Lebanon Foes Approve Peace Talks in Geneva
Artillery Duels Continue in Hills Near Beirut

October 23
Beirut International Airport
0500: A large yellow Mercedes truck enters the public parking area south of the BLT compound, circles once, and then exits the parking lot. It was observed by a sentry, but not reported because it did not stop.

0622: A sudden noise grabbed the attention of Sergeant Steve

Russell, who heard "a sort of popping or crackling sound from the direction of the parking lot." He looked up, hearing the roar of a diesel engine, and a yellow Mercedes stacked-bed truck crashed through the barbed-wire barrier and the chain-link fence. Lance Corporal Eddie DiFranco, manning Post 7, was completely stunned and did not get a clean shot off at the man driving the truck. He ran to radio Sergeant Russell.

A Reconnaissance Platoon leader saw the truck pass twenty-five meters in front of him and was so stunned, he ran and jumped in a nearby rain gutter. Sergeant Russell was now on his feet, next to his guard shack by the building atrium. The truck was moving fast, probably around twenty-five miles per hour. Russell turned toward the atrium and started to run, screaming at a jogger to "Get the fuck out of here!" He ran across the lobby floor and out the back door and yelled "HIT THE DECK!" two or three times.

Russell cut at an angle across the open parking lot and looked back right as the truck flattened the Sergeant of the Guard post. Russell ran another thirty feet or so and turned and looked back for a second time. The truck came to a stop in the center of the BLT atrium lobby.

There appeared to be no movement in the cab discernible to the sergeant. There was extensive damage to the windshield, top, and driver-side door of the truck. The engine had stopped. Sergeant Russell looked at the truck and saw "a bright orange-yellow flash at the grill of the truck" and felt "a wave of intense heat and a powerful concussion."[6]

CHAPTER 9

On a cold, wet Sunday in Syracuse, we were eating dinner when my dad's ear caught something on CNN's Headline News program. The program was not even a year old, and it was the first new format of twenty-four-hour news, to be updated every thirty minutes.

My father got up from the dinner table and walked into the living room—a mortal sin, when we did it. He said, "Oh god, the Marines have been blown up in Beirut!"

My mother dropped her fork and was halfway out of her chair when she yelped, "What did you say? What got blown up?"

My brother and I looked up. I was facing the TV, and could see some of the picture. All I saw was black smoke. Dinner was over.

"The bomb in the bed of the big yellow Mercedes truck consisted of about 12,000 pounds of high explosives wrapped in canisters of flammable gases. It is said to have been the largest non-nuclear blast ever detonated on the face of the earth. Be that as it may, it was placed perfectly within the open atrium lobby of the concrete-and-steel Battalion Landing Team (BLT) headquarters building. The force of the explosion initially lifted the entire four-story structure, shearing the bases of the concrete support columns, each measuring fifteen feet in circumference and reinforced by numerous one-and-three-quarter-inch steel rods. The airborne building then fell in upon itself. A massive shock wave and ball of flaming gas was hurled in all directions. The blast created an oblong crater measuring thirty-nine feet by twenty-nine feet, and eight feet eight inches in depth. This, after shattering the seven-inch-thick steel-reinforced-concrete basement floor."[7]

My mom and dad were glued to the TV for the rest of the night. At that point, they were reporting that something big had happened, an explosion, but they were not sure what did it. My parents went into full panic mode. My mom just kept saying "Oh god." My dad periodically sighed and rubbed his hands. A bomb had just gone off in Beirut and blew up a whole bunch of Marines, and they knew nothing.

After watching the same loop for about two and a half hours and listening to my parents speculate, I got up and went into my room to read, but my parents' worry and anxiety followed me. Watching my parents worry more about Bruce than me was hard. But as we have seen, you get a hand, and you play it. My brother now lived upstairs in Bruce's room, so I had my room to myself. I just read until I fell asleep.

Most of my childhood was an afterthought to my parents. No one asked me how I felt, but it would have been a lie anyway. The large age difference between Bruce, my sister, and me meant that my parents paid more attention to them and what was going on in their world. I was used to it.

When I woke the next morning and got ready to do my route, my dad was sitting on the edge of his chair in his pajamas, lights out, soft glow of a lit cigarette being met with TV glare, watching the news. The ashtray next to him was full, and he looked terrible, extremely tense. There were new pictures since the night before.

"Any word?" I asked, as I stood in my jeans and jacket.

"They believe it was a car bomb," he started off in a raspy voice before clearing his throat. "They say probably over a hundred killed and wounded. It happened where most of the guys sleep. I'm not sure if Bruce was there. They hit the French also." He let out a big sigh and flicked his cigarette in the ashtray, kicking off the ash then tamping down the tip.

I had absolutely no idea what to say. My dad was watching TV, hoping to see Bruce dash across the screen, or see his head pop up, or see him carried out of the wreckage on a stretcher, or see his body stuck in rubble, only to watch him die.

"Alright, Pop, it will be okay" was all I could muster. *I just reassured my father that the brother who abused me would be okay.* My head still spins thinking about it. I may have been indifferent about what happened to Bruce, but I did not want to see my parents struggle.

I headed out the door into the cold, foggy morning. When I got my papers, the headline read 174 dead in terrorist attack. Wow! That was crazy to read. This was not a dumbass John Wayne movie. This was real-life US soldiers getting blown to shit. The picture showed a black soldier in his boxers, covered in dust, being carried out of a pile of rubble—the Battalion Landing headquarters that used to exist there.

I folded the paper up and went about my deliveries. The world seemed different that day. The usual routine seemed to shift a little. Lights were already on in houses where they usually were not. It was my first time watching people experience a disaster like this. It affected my family, but it also affected the country.

When I got home from my route, everyone was up. My dad had gotten dressed, and my mom was eating breakfast while watching TV; she looked like she hadn't slept. My dad had decided not to go to work that day, staying home just in case there was a call, or a car. A call to tell them Bruce was alive and maybe wounded. A car to tell them he was not alive and the Marines have come to tell us.

I got showered, ate breakfast, and got ready for school. By this time, I had started walking the other way to school by myself, a five-minute walk. My parents' nervousness was electric as I left the house. They were a million miles away.

At school, the teachers were all a-buzz with the news. In homeroom, PS (whom I had told earlier in the year that Bruce was in Beirut) was consoling. We chatted a little about it. As seventh graders, we were trying to process this international action involving our military, not to mention our own personal ties to it.

After school I had a new afternoon paper route. I went

right home after school. My dad was standing, watching TV. I walked in and asked what was up.

"No word yet, no one has called and no one has come by."

I put my backpack away and got a quick snack, then went into the living room and watched the news with my dad. He floated between his chair and the front window.

The front page of the evening paper was all Beirut.

Monday, October 24
Massacre in Beirut
Stunned Marines Regroup
Reagan Retreat and No Escalation
(Picture) A Marine is carried on a stretcher across the rubble of the BLT bombing. The pictures show chaos and destruction. Eight Marines are pictured at the top of the page; Bruce's tank-chew picture was used, but just a head/shoulder shot. They are the eight Marines from the previous Syracuse-area article.

My parents were not alone in their pain and fear. But I was caught right in the middle of it all, just trying to figure it all out on my own, as usual.

My mom was home when I arrived. She was a bundle of nerves just like my dad. They had nowhere to go, trapped by the TV and the phone. Waiting for some news, any news. I did not know what to say or do.

My sister popped her head in and stayed for dinner that night, helped to talk my mom off the ledge. Neither of my parents were doing mentally well over this, and I could not blame them. They were not sleeping or eating, but they were chain-smoking. Sitting at home to hear if your child has been blown up is not an ideal situation to be stuck in.

I had sympathy for the "if-then" world they were now residing in. I had been a resident for a period of time—fucking mayor at one point—of the "if-then" community. My whole life was one big "if-then" situation, based around my own survival.

Tuesday, October 25
Waiting
"The hardest part is just not knowing." —My father

Wednesday, October 26
Not Knowing Marines' Fate Hardest Part

Thursday, October 27
Good News for 2; Others Keep Vigil
My father informed the press that he spoke to a spokesman for the Marines and it appeared Bruce was not near the blast. He got the call that afternoon at 4:30 p.m.

"I'm starting to spread my wings a little bit. Maybe tomorrow I'll be soaring like an eagle." —Bruce Herbig, Sr.

Friday, October 28
And Now There Are Just 2 to Hear From
Article references that some families of Marines had been notified that their son is alive, but two families had not.

I woke up Saturday morning to do the usual route. This was my last morning-delivery, ever. Going forward, I would just deliver papers at night. I dressed warmly, because I could hear the wind outside.

In the living room, my dad was watching TV. "Hey Pop, what's up?"

"Bruce called," he said with a big smile on his face. "He's alive. He was 1,000 yards away, at the other end of the airport, when the blast went off. He said they got word to man the tanks and surround the perimeter of the blast site. Said they were taking some sniper fire, but were allowed to return fire."

"Alright, Dad, that's great news. I told you it would be fine." I threw on my jacket and headed out the door. "Go get some sleep. I'll be back in a bit."

"Be safe," he said as I was closing the door.

I thought to myself, *For you, Dad, I'll be safe.*

My dad did not care about the headline in the morning paper that day. He already knew the truth. He did not need to know anything except that Bruce was alive.

My parents were through the roof. A big part of their anxiety and fear was lifted; the dark cloud that was floating in the house finally floated away. They called my grandmother and told her. I had not seen her all week; this was not something big enough for her to actually come over and see how my parents were.

So, Bruce was alive, but he was still in Beirut. That had not changed.

School was okay; it was good to see PS each morning. He grew on me—very sharp kid, with a good, dry sense of humor. He was into music and we would talk the Doors and the Grateful Dead. I was meeting new kids here and there, but none were Garrett or Dan. To be fair, I was measuring these new people with an unfair measuring stick—deciding what they were not, instead of what they could be.

About a week into November, my dad asked me at the dinner table, "How's school?"

I just sat there for a second and thought, *It's going on the middle of November and I have been full of anxiety, going to a new school with no friends. I'm afraid to come home because my parents are terrified that their oldest son is in a war zone and being bombed and shot at. Three girls at school make fun of me because I wear hand-me-down clothes and I am just trying to find a place to exist, hoping that my secret never gets out. I miss Garrett and Dan and the security they provided me.*

"It's okay, found all my classes and trying to meet new people. It's fine." The magic words: *It's fine. I am fine. Everyone is fine.*

My parents knew Bruce would be coming home soon, they

just didn't know when. On the nightly news it was announced: the 24th MAU would be leaving Beirut the morning of November 19, heading to Rota, Spain, and then back home to Camp Lejeune, North Carolina.

I met a girl at school and we talked on the phone a lot. I liked her—and she was the first female outside my family that I had experienced affection for. The simmering soup of puberty! It felt good to be liked and appreciated by someone I liked. I even kissed her—my first. School had taken a new turn, even if everything else still sucked.

I spent time talking to her on the phone and doing what seventh-graders do in their early relationships: hope you don't fuck it up. We would spend time together here and there after school. Such a weird time in life; especially when you don't have any clue what you're doing and have no one to talk to about it. In some ways she added to my anxiety, because I was fearful of doing anything to hurt the relationship. Instead of finding out about her and telling her about me, I was thinking about how to avoid my secret. A not-very-healthy way to start a relationship. I was so afraid of what of what she would think of me. It was nice to be liked by someone who didn't expect me to mow the lawn.

November 27
Upstate Families Watch Changing of the Guard an Ocean Away
Article referencing the 24th MAU coming home and local parents expecting their sons to come home. My mom is quoted saying she believes Bruce is going to come home for two weeks during Christmas.

The snow started—nothing crazy, just a few inches the first couple weeks of December. School was marginally getting better, the more people I got to know. My parents' expectations to have Bruce home for Christmas were dashed when he said that he could not come home, he had used up his leave in Italy. My parents were super bummed; I think they really wanted to see him and see how he was, not the lip service the Marines and he were giving them.

I was indifferent on the matter. Bruce could come or go. I had no say, so all I could do was play my cards and shut up. Children should be seen, not heard. I was definitely becoming more isolated from my family, but it was normal to me; it had always been that way.

Christmas came and Bruce was affecting it yet again, but not in his usual felonious fashion. My parents wanted to see him and make sure he was well, and it was visibly hard on them not to be able to. Luckily, my sister was there to bring good tidings and inappropriate behavior. As much as she tried to lift my parents' spirits, I could tell they were a thousand miles away.

I made it through the holidays and into the second half of seventh grade. It was now 1984 and George Orwell was all the buzz.

The girl of my dreams, the one I would marry and live with for eternity—we broke up. Young love (*it hurts so much, the pain!!!!!!!*) comes and goes so fast. But I now had a couple of guys I was hanging out with, though I still reserved as much weekend time with Garrett and Dan as I could.

Bruce wrote home that he was okay. He had to go to some training in February or March and then would be returning back to Camp Lejeune. My parents were worried about him. He said he did counseling that all the Marines were required to do, but didn't really elaborate on anything.

We got through the last months of winter: January, February, and March. I much preferred having a nighttime than a morning paper route in the winter, that was for sure. In the morning, no one has shoveled the snow and it is usually the coldest.

I went out for the track team in the spring. It was a good time and I met a couple of people that way. I really liked running, it suited me. I ended up running the half-mile, which was perfect for me. I genuinely loved that race. It was great to practice and race, and I was decent at it. We ran five races or so against other middle schools and I came in first for three races and second for two. I always felt so great from head to toe after a race/practice; like my mind and body were smooth machines. Some of the students I ran with would go on to track careers at our high school and do very well with the sport. I was not one of them.

I would practice track at the high school, or run a meet, and then deliver my papers. The end of my route brought me right back to my doorstep. I was getting better sleep since I joined track, but it was still erratic at times, my mind racing at night, not falling asleep until after 1 or 2 a.m. Sometimes I woke up with my mind spinning with thoughts. I would go out and watch TV, pretending I just got up and turned on the TV a second ago when my dad got up. Erratic sleep would follow me through the rest of my life.

In the middle of May, the phone rang at about 9 p.m. at night. I got up to answer it, said "Hello," and heard my name in a loud, mumbled bark.

"What, hello? Bruce? Is that you?"

"Fuck you, motherfucker! Put Dad on the phone, you son of a bitch. I wanna talk to that asshole!"

He was clearly drunk. I called my dad over and told him it was Bruce, and he was drunk and very angry.

As soon as my dad said hello, I heard Bruce at the top of his lungs just explicitly cut into my dad: "motherfucker" this and "go fuck yourself" that. My dad was trying to get a word in edgewise, begging Bruce to listen, but he got nowhere, and then suddenly the line was dead.

My father looked at the phone and then hung it up, a look of despair on his face. He explained to my mother what had happened and what was said. They had sent a letter to Bruce's company chaplain and given him a call a few weeks back to check on Bruce. He had fallen off their radar, had not written in a while or called home. I guess Bruce did not want to be checked up on. They now had Bruce's response. Me too!

CHAPTER 10

At the beginning of June, track season was about over and school would be ending soon. My year in public school had ended with some new cool friends and a sport I liked. All in all, it was turning out to be bearable. We had a final track meet at Nottingham High and then one more race at Henninger High, the school across the city where my other brother went to school because my parents did not want him around any of Bruce's influences.

The first Tuesday of June, after practice I headed over this guy JP's house, in the neighborhood. People hung out there and played basketball. I played a game or two before heading up the street to do my route. I could feel spring moving into summer: it was cool out, but with big bubbles of warm air drifting through.

The dark sedan pulled up in front of the brick-bottom house and two gentlemen got out of the car. They both affixed their white covers on their heads, black brims down to their eyebrows, then a quick pull up for proper placement. The driver was carrying a black attaché.

They walked briskly up the sidewalk, up the two steps, and looked at the door, which was partially ajar, the screen closed. They rang the doorbell, and loud barks rang out. Both men took a step back. "Be quiet, be quiet" they heard from the inside.

A short, round middle-aged woman answered the door, with a loud barking black dog at her heels. "Hello," she said. The Marines stared at the woman and introduced themselves.

I filed this scene away in my mind, got my papers, finished up my route, and headed home. I was glad the year was ending. It had been a tough year for me. At times I'd felt lost and the anxiety was tough to deal with—crippling during the end of October when the bombing went down. I felt very alone without Garrett and Dan. My parents went through some very hard times, things I could not understand as a child.

I walked up my street, paying no attention to the dark sedan in front of my house. As I walked up the steps I heard a commotion inside. I opened the screen door, and pushed the front door open. In front of me was my sister.

She took me by both arms, sat me down on the couch, and sat down next to me. She looked right at me.

"Bruce is dead. He killed himself. You need to go over and see Mom."

I just looked at her quizzically. "What?"

She repeated what she'd said. The reason I was having a hard time processing it was because of the very loud noise coming from the dining room: a noise of anger, and pain, and fear. The noise was my mother wailing because she had just lost her eldest son. It was a noise I never want to hear again as long as I live.

I hugged my sister, whose face was as confused as I have ever seen it. As I got up and walked toward the dining room, the wails became louder. At the dining room table, our neighbor, LR, was sitting in my dad's spot. My mom was in her chair, with a box of Kleenex, glasses off, hysterical. Sitting to her left, a Marine in his dress-blue uniform nodded to me as I entered the room. His partner sat next to him in my seat, and also nodded to me. The same two I had seen earlier.

I went and kneeled at my mom's chair. I had never seen her so upset, even at her parents' funerals. She was sobbing into my shoulder and I said I was sorry. I had nothing else to say.

After a few minutes I looked up and realized that neither my brother nor my dad were home. I got up and walked into the living room, a shitload of emotions washing over me. I was twelve years old. I wandered around my living room for a few minutes, my emotional load much different from my mom's and sister's.

I went into my room and must have sat on my bed and got up and walked to the door about thirty times. My mind was spinning in a hundred different directions. I heard my brother come home and I walked out to the dining room. He was with my mom, whose wailing started up again when she saw him. I hugged him and he walked into the living room and sat down.

Dad! In the dining room, my dad and mom were hugging. My dad was clearly upset and crying; he grabbed me and hugged me for a few minutes. My mom and dad were crushed beyond belief.

The next few hours were an emotional shit show, everyone in a different place emotionally. I slipped back to my room and hung out there for a couple hours, as my parents called family and friends. No one noticed that I was not really around. They never really did. The house was full of people from 6 p.m. until late into the night, the phone ringing and calls being made.

I spent the next few hours just kind of moving between things. People came over to console my parents and my sister was on the phone with relatives. I was having conversations on autopilot, trying to get the gist of what was happening with the funeral.

Garrett's parents showed up, and my mom talked to Garrett's mom by the front door, motioning me to her. Garrett's mom passed along her condolences. My mom said, "For the funeral, you, Garrett, and Dan will serve as the altar boys, okay?"

I nodded, but my heart just sunk. I was taken aback by the proposition but unable to refuse. *Wow, front-row seats to the show I never wanted to see.* I wanted no part in the process of burying Bruce, he did not deserve my time or energy. I did not give a fuck that Bruce was dead.

How was I supposed to feel? What should my reaction have been? I don't know. I didn't want him to die, but I was more than willing to accept this new card into my hand and play it. His death meant that he could not physically hurt me again.

Back in the kitchen, my dad was talking to my neighbor, PD. I walked in and they were finishing up a conversation.

"Bruce, I'm going to the store, need anything?" PD asked.

My dad replied no, but I quickly butted in. "Chocolate ice cream, please."

After I said that, I went to my room and got a couple bucks off my dresser, went back out, holding the money out to PD. He looked at me and waved it off. "Put that away. I probably owe you money for watching my kids."

Not long after, PD walked through the front door with a white plastic bag and handed the half-gallon of Sealtest chocolate ice cream to me. I grabbed a spoon and walked out to the front porch. It was a warm night for that time of year; I ate the ice cream in a T-shirt and shorts.

My head was all mixed up. I never wanted Bruce dead. I hated him for what he did, but I didn't want him dead. I definitely didn't want him to commit suicide. It would have been better if he'd died in Beirut. That at least could be explained; a suicide cannot be explained, especially when there is no note.

I stood out there on the porch by myself, eating ice cream. I knew that at school nobody would know, but since we had just been in the paper and my dad did a live TV interview on our fucking lawn, the press would know soon. And so would everyone else. It had all come down to this.

I had no idea where it would end. I knew I could never say anything about the abuse now, at least not anytime soon. I was out of danger and I didn't have to worry about him anymore.

I sat on the side of my porch and looked at the stars. No clouds.

When I woke up around 6 a.m., everyone was still asleep. Felt like Christmas morning, creeping out before everyone was awake. I was going to school today, I decided. I could not see myself sitting around all day with my family.

I crept through the day like any other without tipping my hand, missing Garrett and Dan. I did our last track meet and finished second in my race; plus, we won as a team. That day's paper didn't have anything in it about Bruce.

At home I met the Marine who had accompanied Bruce's body back, Sergeant HB—a gentleman the size of a house who was a real nice guy, very attentive to my parents. He was Bruce's sergeant back at Camp Lejeune, in town for the next few days to help my parents.

I went to school the next day feeling okay. I'd had a decent night's sleep, considering. At school I just tried to keep my emotions in check; between the abuse and the suicide, I had so much swirling around my head. At track practice I told my coach that I wouldn't be able to make practice the next day because I needed to attend a funeral.

June 7
Syracuse Marine Who Survived Beirut Bombing Found Dead

The headline ripped across the front of the evening paper, along with a picture of Bruce. They used a cropped photo of the tank picture with him grabbing chew—my mother was pissed about that. I had to carry my newspapers with the headline facing away because I just could not keep seeing it. As I finished up my route, I felt no real urge to go home. Relatives were starting to roll in, to console my mom and dad.

At home, I said hello to the appropriate people and felt my space being invaded again. I gave the paper to my dad and left him in his chair as I went off to shower. No one in my family ever asked me about delivering all those papers with Bruce's article on the front page. I knew that the article meant that everyone in school the next day was going to know.

Everything happening at home had just been pushed to the side. The more aunts, uncles, and cousins that showed up, the more I slipped into the shadows. Large, complicated adult conversations were going on, plus there was family drama afoot. My cousin T, one of C's brothers, was coming for the funeral all the way from Hawai'i, where he was stationed in the Navy. T wanted to marry his high school sweetheart, but his parents—and now by extension, all the adult family members—did not think that was a good idea. So, beyond putting Bruce in the ground, there was a marriage that was being prevented. I was getting sick and tired of listening to the "adults" in the room telling the younger generation shit. *How about this? Everyone above the age of thirty, shut the fuck up!*

(By the way, cousin T and said wife have two beautiful daughters and a beautiful granddaughter to boot. They are still married and adults of the '80s are idiots.)

It seemed there was a fucking person in my way every time I turned around. I got to school late the next morning, with all the chaos in the house.

As I opened the door to school and walked in, heads began to turn, conversations petering off into silence. *Maybe this wasn't a good idea.* Students were looking at me, teachers were looking at me. It hit me like a punch to the chest, but I wouldn't let myself show any emotion.

As I walked to my locker, I mostly kept my eyes down, made eye contact with a few people and stopped at their locker to receive their condolences. Nobody ever said the wrong thing or was impolite about the situation. I just felt like the biggest sore thumb because I didn't know anyone other than the people on my academic team. Now they all knew this big, hard thing about me. It was much harder than I thought it would be.

My dad picked me up right after lunch and a big weight lifted off my body, to be replaced by others. We went home and I got washed up and changed.

There were two viewings, 2–4 p.m. and 7–9 p.m., plus I had to deliver my papers in between sessions. I had cousins at my neighbors', my grandmother's house, a local hotel—they were everywhere. We got to the funeral home a little early to watch the casket arrive.

Four Marine honor guards were there to receive it and they would stand over the casket during calling hours. They placed an American flag over the casket and it was wheeled inside and placed in a receiving room. My mom imploded and a couple people had to catch her. That wail was back again and it sent a visceral shot down my spine, into my stomach.

People started showing up: Garrett's parents, Dan's parents, and other friends of my parents. Two of the four honor guard stood at Bruce's coffin, one on either side, facing each other. When someone approached the coffin, they would snap to attention. Once the person retreated, they went back to at-ease.

Calling hours were full of lots of crying and consoling. After about forty-five minutes I went downstairs to the reception room to get some water. It was beginning to wear on me, people coming up and consoling me. There was nothing wrong with what they were saying per se, but the words of consolation didn't apply to me. He was dead and I was safe. I didn't have real regrets he was dead, but of course I knew my parents did. It was a confusing day, but all those days were. I was biding my time, while everyone else, except my brother and sister, grieved.

After the first viewing was over, we headed home for food and water. Death is very dehydrating. I changed and went to deliver my papers. When I came home, the house was in chaos. There were relatives and friends of the family everywhere: the front porch, inside, and the back patio. I remember coming home, saying hello to people, going in my room and crawling into bed for about twenty minutes. I was burnt-out, like I was expending a vast amount of energy, but I hadn't really exercised. Everything felt harder, mentally and physically.

Then I sucked it up and went out and joined everyone. We ate before we left for the second session. My track coach showed up, which was very nice of him.

I remember being at the funeral home for about a half-hour, and my mom said we could go home early. My brother and I and a couple of my cousins were cut loose and dropped at home.

I changed and decompressed a little, knowing the calm wouldn't last long; it was going to get crazy again around 9:15 p.m.

Everything was moving so fast, and it was surreal, every-one very emotional—then there I was, just sort of dispassionate to my surroundings. One thing I didn't want to do, that I men-tally said to myself was, *Don't stick out. Don't give anyone any reason to question beyond being or not being "sad."* I felt like I didn't fit in, that I was visiting the situation. I had decided that there was absolutely no reason to tell anyone about the abuse now. I was finally safe from Bruce, so there was nothing to worry about anymore.

Around 9:15, people started to come home. My mom must have drunk about five glasses of water. She was hurting a lot. My dad muddled through; he just sighed and looked distant. I think he really wanted to shrink into himself, but there was too much going on. The adults hung out drinking, my sister stayed over to make morning logistics run smoother. I hung out for a little while talking with people, then went to my room. It took me a long time to unwind from the day's events, which had felt like a month rolled up into twenty-four hours. I was very over-whelmed and extremely anxious.

I woke up before my alarm, around 5:30 a.m., peered out of my room and saw the bathroom was free, and ducked in. I showered and changed. My family and a few others were going to the funeral home, where the Marine guard would remove the casket, place it in the hearse, and escort it to the church.

I hung out by myself for the first time in what seemed like months, and then I walked over to the church and met Garrett and Dan.

First words out of Garrett's mouth were "Does anyone remember how to perform the altar boy job?" We had a good chuckle.

I was pissed I had to perform this religious ceremony for the person who abused me. But realistically the Catholic church was familiar with such situations, even if the general public at large didn't know their secrets.

Upstairs, we started to put all the religious tchotchkes out for the ceremony. A funeral meant incense, and I was sure that neither my brother nor my mother had taken any allergy pills.

It was hard being in that church. I had thought I was done with Catholicism; being pulled off the bench to come in and sub was rough. Garrett and I walked around setting things out, and Dan came behind us and corrected what we messed up.

As people started to show up, we were in the back room waiting for the starting gun. I knew when my mother had arrived because I could hear her cry. Suddenly, my sister popped her head in. TK, our friend the priest, was conducting the ceremony and my sister was reading the eulogy—so no one could get up there and say how great Bruce was and he would be missed. They talked logistics for a second and then she came over to us and thanked the guys.

Finally, 9:30 a.m. rolled around, and like every live show, it is going to happen whether you're ready or not. The funeral started and no one rose from the dead.

As TK was going through some opening remarks, I heard the rear door of the church open with its familiar squeak. I was seated farthest from the aisle, so I had to poke my head around Dan and Garrett to see who it was. I saw my sister's head turn too; she was on the aisle, so she could easily go up for her eulogy. She and I would later talk about who this person was.

He looked like Jim Morrison—but not the young, slender, charismatic Jim Morrison. I mean the fat, unkempt, Soft Parade days. He was barefoot and wore jeans, T-shirt, leather vest, and a large-brimmed leather hat. He looked like he could be the bassist for Stevie Ray Vaughan's Double Trouble band. My sister and I believe it was JH, a longtime running partner of Bruce's and, apparently, his only friend left.

The rest of the funeral went along as usual. My mother and brother, who are highly allergic to incense, looked like a couple of snotty chipmunks by the end. The service was humiliating for me but I was so very glad to be doing it with my friends. They made the whole day bearable.

We wrapped things up fairly quickly after the ceremony, and I made my way out front to get a ride. MK, a friend of my parents (later my French tutor), drove me to the cemetery.

There, I joined my sister, who was with a whole gaggle of people, waiting for the casket to be removed and the pallbearers to take hold of the casket and proceed to the grave-site. She and I interlocked arms and started to walk over. It was sunny, with a little breeze, warm for early June. We walked over to the site and gathered around the hole as the casket was laid down.

If you stand at the end of Garrett's driveway and look at 1 o'clock, you can see the cemetery. We used to ride our bikes up the dirt road and, when we were younger, we would follow the stream that ran along Meadowbrook, which cut through the cemetery, and skip rocks. This was the second time I had been in the cemetery for business. As we walked to the site, we passed by my grandfather's plot, the one who died when I was two.

After everyone had arrived, TK, who had presided over the service, began to give his graveside prayers and words to the family. When he finished, he motioned to the Marine guard, who commenced the firing of the twenty-one-gun salute. I could feel the tension rise.

Next, the bugler stepped forward and put the instrument to his lips, and blew the first opening notes of "Taps"—sounding like someone trying to strangle a seal. My sister and I hugged our arms tight, put our heads down, and we both snarfed, trying to hold in our laughs. About fifty eyes immediately popped up and looked at us, my mother and father included. The next three notes came out and a couple more snarfs and a minor snort were heard from the cousin gallery.

Needless to say, my sister and I kept our heads down. You could hear the laughter being held back, even from some of the adults. By the end, the Marine in charge of the salute had a look of "just fucking end" in his eyes. It was a needed moment of hilarity, because now came the hard part.

Two Marines removed the American flag that was draped on Bruce's coffin. They folded the flag in half lengthwise, stripes to stars, and then folded it again. The Marine holding the stripes then folded the flag in a triangle, so the bottom part met the long part of the flag, and kept repeating this until the stripes met the stars and the last piece was folded in, exposing the stars on top. The Marine holding the stars then took the flag, spun on his heel, and stood at full attention in front of my mother and father. He bent at the waist to my mother, with one hand above and one hand below the flag, and said in a low voice, "On behalf of the President of the United States, the United States Marine Corps, and a gr—"

My mother lost it. You could not hear the rest of what was said because of my mother crying. My father took the flag from him, nodded his appreciation, and placed it on my mom's hands. My mother's scream was the loudest I've heard in my entire life, louder even than the guy who had boiling water poured on his leg.

TK said some more words, then relayed that people were coming to our house afterward. The graveside ceremony ended, and my sister and I got a ride back to our house, where I changed into shorts and a T-shirt. It was unusually warm the whole week.

A friend of our family's from church had stayed back at our house and gotten things ready for people to come over. She had everything set up when we got home.

A half-hour later, after people had a drink at the bar, they began to show up. My cousins came right over after they changed and started drinking. The Marines ended up at a picnic table that our neighbor had brought over, in the driveway. The six of them were given a Matt's Beer Ball, a five-gallon plastic ball of beer that came with a special tap, created and distributed by Matt Brewery. It's America, damn it!

The grill was rolling and there were platters of food. I spent the first few hours with Garrett and Dan, which helped me a lot. During this time, each of my aunts, uncles, and cousins came over and thanked the Marines for participating in the ceremony that day. They also made sure to shake the hand of the bugle player and personally thanked him for his playing. No harm, no foul, my friend.

At around 3 p.m., a family friend came barreling around the house and headed right for the picnic table and the Marines. "Get up, move! Come with me," he barked.

All the men stopped their talking, put their beers down, and got up and followed him to where three adults were coming down the driveway.

"Nope, nope get the fuck out! I don't give a damn if you're a reporter, they do not want to speak you."

The lead reporter stepped up and talked to HB in a low tone. A bunch of people were watching.

"They do not want to talk to you. Period!" HB responded.

The three people stood there for a second and then turned around and went back to their car. HB and the Marines watched the car pull away, and then HB turned around with a big grin and said, "As you were, men," and back to the beer they went.

I took off about a half-hour later to go deliver my papers. The only thing written about Bruce that day was a tiny obit in the deaths section. My parents didn't want to put out anything else after everything that had been written.

By the time I got home, people were leaving. The Marines were gone, the Beer Ball crushed. Garrett and Dan took off soon after I got home, with their parents. Then it was pretty much my family and extended drinking. After a while, a group, led by my sister, got in cabs to go to a bar. After they left, things died down considerably. My cousins sleeping next door went and crashed because they would need to be up early to leave. My aunt, uncle, and younger cousin went back to my grandmother's house.

It was over. It had been a very long week. I was full of mixed emotions and I felt like I could not process any of them; my brain couldn't pick one. I could not even read, I was so wound up; the words just seemed to bounce off my eyes. It took a long while of just listening to the radio to relax.

I turned off the light, listened to the music, and looked out my window onto the backyard. I could still smell barbecue and beer. I just looked into the darkness, like I had a thousand nights before. Like the night he abused me. I could hear the bats flap in the backyard, eating the mosquitoes.

I always found answers in the dark, and sometimes safety. But this night, none came.

I was safe and alone. The situation with Bruce was over and the story behind him and me was buried with him.

I had a hard time sleeping. I don't remember falling asleep, but I didn't hear my sister or cousins come in.

I woke about 6 a.m. the next morning, and came out to find people already milling about, regretting the booze of the night before. My cousins packed up and said goodbye. My sister made breakfast. I remember going on the front porch and getting the Sunday paper, and finding nothing else written about Bruce or my family.

After breakfast, the house just hung with grief, emanating from my parents. It made it hard to be inside. We spent the morning saying goodbye to relatives.

Late-morning, I grabbed my bike and took off. My sister and parents were sitting around talking and I just wasn't feeling it. I took off for Barry Park to get some energy out. I got to the park and went toward the pond and the jogging trail. I rode my bike along the trail, just trying to expend as much energy as possible. I was probably at the park for an hour or so before I headed home. I felt a little relief, but nowhere near what I needed.

HB came by and picked up me and my brother. My brother is not much of a talker, so I could not tell you how he was feeling, but I imagine he was happy not to have the menace of Bruce around anymore. I never felt the need to ask my siblings how they felt, because I was beside them the whole time. We were better off as a family now. Safer, at least.

HB took us on a short drive across town. We pulled up in front of a brick building with a barbed-wire-topped fence around it—the local armory. HB got out of the car and told us to wait.

He came back in a few minutes with another gentleman,

who stuck his head in the car and passed along his condolences. HB got in the car and drove around the building to the back lot, where he parked the car right next an M1A1 battle tank, the same model Bruce had used in Beirut.

We got out and gazed over the outside of the tank. The man who HB met came out of a side door and yelled over to us, "Go ahead and climb up and in if you want."

So, my brother and I, curious, proceeded to climb up onto the battle tank. It was big and mean. It was quite a bit of machinery, hard to explain or imagine until you personally see it.

I climbed down into and sat in the driver's seat, with the controls in front of me. I asked for the keys, but I imagine the gentlemen outside didn't hear, or ignored me.

The other gentleman stuck his head in the hatch and gave a quick rundown of the tank: speed, forward and reverse, diameter of main gun and its ordinance capabilities, type of machine gun on the turret and its capabilities, rounds fired per second and effective range. He told us about its fuel consumption (not good!) and other specifications of that particular model.

He also briefly explained Bruce's duties as the loader. Each tank member carried a sidearm, except for the loader, who had a sidearm and access to the only M16 on board.

After a half-hour or so, we left. We thanked the gentleman for the invite and tour and HB personally thanked him for the favor, then dropped us off at home.

At home, my sister told me she was bolting after dinner to get back to the real world. Around 4:30 p.m. or so, our doorbell rang, and I got up to answer it. As I pulled back the open front door to the screen, in front of me was a woman carrying a big box.

"Hi, can I help you?" I asked.

"Hi, ah, how are you?" she said to me with a blank face, looking for words. "I made this for you because I thought you folks wouldn't be up to cooking."

I opened the screen door and the smell of the cooked turkey overtook the front foyer. She was holding a cardboard box that was a little bit bigger than a turkey, which she handed to me. "There are potatoes in there, gravy, green beans, and some dinner rolls. Sorry, I didn't have time to bake anything for dessert."

I looked up at her in disbelief and amazement. I had never seen this woman before. "Thank you, thank you very much," I said. She smiled and walked off the porch.

I walked into the living room, everyone's eyes on me. "Who was that? What is that?" I explained and said I needed to put it down before I dropped it. Something was beginning to emanate heat into my forearm. My dad got up, looked it over, then went to the porch. After a second he came back in and said, "She's gone."

I placed the box on the kitchen counter and started to open it up. I had not had lunch and I was hungry as shit. I fixed myself a full plate: turkey, potatoes, beans, stuffing, and some gravy. I was so happy, and sat at the dining room table, contently by myself. People started to drift in and pick at the food, eventually joining me at the table. I guess they'd all forgotten to eat lunch too. It was the first full meal for the five of us at the table without Bruce. We ate in silence.

I just got up when I was done. It was the first time I ever got up from my dad's table without asking permission.

I got to school the next day and everything was back to normal. I still felt odd walking the halls, with everyone knowing such intimate stuff about me. It felt like they knew a secret about me that I didn't. We had track practice, with just one last meet to go, a city-wide meet at Henninger on Friday.

Friday was the last full day of school. My mother had told me that she and my brother would be at the race. It was hot again that afternoon.

When it came time for the half-mile we lined up. This was the first time I was running on a rubberized track in my life and it felt great. Instead of the usual four or five of us running the race there would be six runners—which was fine by me.

We got set, then *bang!* The pistol went off and we started. I started about fifth and moved my way up to second quickly. This was a short race, so any moves needed to be made early. I was pushing the first lap and staying right in the corner of the lead kid's right eye.

After we completed the first lap and rounded the bottom turn, I could feel every blood cell just give up its oxygen. My body started to slow down, no matter how hard I pushed. All my energy was just suddenly gone, I was fading. Third place....fourth. I could hear people scream my name: "Pete, run, run, Pete, run!" But I had nothing. Fifth place... We were rounding the top curve and I literally had nothing left for the last hundred yards. Sixth place... I finished dead last by a couple of lengths.

I walked forward, trying to catch my breath. I didn't want to speak to anyone. I felt like such a loser. To blow it like that in front of all my teammates and my mom and brother was just plain humiliating. I tried my very best not to be upset in front of anyone.

We finished up the rest of the events and ended the meet. On the way to the car, my brother told me I ran a good race, which must have taken a lot for him to say because I knew he would rather be anywhere else in the world other than that track.

I got in the car and was silent all the way home. I got out, went inside to drop my school things, and went to deliver my papers. I never ran track again.

HB had eaten dinner with us that whole week. When my mom found out he was eating McDonald's every night for dinner, she freaked out. He stayed away on Sunday afternoon, calling my dad to check in, then showed up on Monday night around 5 p.m. On Friday when I got home from deliveries, HB was there, along with my mom.

I jumped in the shower and threw on sweats and a T-shirt.

It had finally cooled down a bit, since our early June heat wave. My dad came home, then my brother. We all ate dinner together and hung out. HB was heading back to Camp Lejeune, so he and my dad spent the night talking.

CHAPTER 11

The rest of the school year finished up, with half-days and finals. We played basketball after school and the days warmed up again. I knew it was not going to be a summer like in the past—I would be on to new adventures.

My next-door neighbors owned a camp up in the Thousand Islands, and they had asked my parents if I wanted to come up there and watch their kids for a couple of weeks and make some money. Then my parents pretty much told me that this was what I would be doing.

It was the exact opposite of what I wanted to do. I was really stressed and wanted to hang out with Garrett and Dan. I didn't want to go to some isolated place, with no friends and no one to talk to. But my objections fell on deaf ears and by the end of June I was gone. I had to quit my paper route.

It was a fine enough time up in the Thousand Islands, swimming, fishing, and canoeing. The family was terrific and their kids were great, but every time I had a thought to myself, or a moment alone, my thoughts were back in Syracuse with the boys. I wanted to be with them, hanging out, and talking about stupid, goofy 13-year-old boy stuff. (That is a whole different book, not to be written by me.) I wanted to play basketball, ride bikes, play football, and maybe even go to the park and ride around the pond. One half of me was fine, the other half was completely miserable. There was no way to tell anyone what I wanted or needed, so I just kept figuring things out by myself.

By the beginning of August, I was home with Garrett and Dan, trying to scare up games to play. If there was nothing going on, I would ride my bike over to Garrett's and spend the day with him, goofing off or playing chess. It was exactly what I needed.

And then, toward the end of August, my parents took my sister to college. She was pretty damn excited—I was not. I had never been this far away from my sister before. She and I spent a lot of time together and she looked out for me. When my parents were busy trying to save Bruce, she was there for me whenever she could be. I was sad to see her leave and be so far away. It made life at home hard for me, one of my safeties gone. I knew my mom would miss her, because my sister helped my mom a lot after Bruce's death.

But ultimately, my dad missed my sister the most. He moped for a while after they got back from dropping her off. He was very proud of my sister for how hard she worked to get where she got (except gym).

September, and school started back up. Everywhere you went, all you heard was Prince's *Purple Rain.* Everyone wanted to dance in the purple rain.

I didn't have nearly as much anxiety as I had the year before. This time around, I knew people walking in, I knew the school and the teachers. Best thing about a seventh-and-eighth-grade middle school: you go from zero to hero in a year. I joined the soccer team in the fall, which opened me up to meeting new people, both in my grade and the grade below, some of whom I'm still in touch with to this day.

The one drawback was I was still with the same group of kids who knew I was the kid whose brother shot himself, which made me more insecure.

Still, school was a lot easier socially in eighth grade. I felt more at ease, but I was still on guard. A flirt or a joke was always my best defense and I tried to use both to my advantage whenever I felt someone was getting uncomfortably personal. I would hone that skill in the years to come.

In October, my mom and dad told me I was going to be attending a Hope for Bereaved meeting. The nonprofit, based in Syracuse, helps people get through their grief of death, with free programs. My parents had been going to weekly meetings for a few weeks. Now, they thought I would benefit from these meetings—though not my brother. I wondered why he got a pass.

After much debate, disagreement, and disgruntlement I went to the event to get my parents off my back. It was held at a private Catholic school near Barry Park.

We entered the classroom and there were about six other people there; my parents nodded at a few of them. My anxiety was through the roof and I had no desire to be in that room with those people.

Now, I'm not against reputable therapy, or therapy groups. I feel people should take the necessary steps to keep themselves and their loved ones happy and safe, and sometimes therapy can help with that. As humans, we are only capable of very limited self-healing. We cry when we are sad, and we can heal a scratch or a bruise by ourselves to help heal small wounds—but cannot heal compound fractures, or open chest wounds. In those situations, or when dealing with anxiety, schizophrenia, or depression, we need real, qualified medical help.

The real problem was this was the wrong group for me. I belonged down the hall in a whole different group, dealing with a whole other problem. I went to three of these group meetings, and each one pissed me off more. The moderator could tell I was pissed and did little to provoke me, although I knew certain things he said were meant for me.

Around this time, a friend of my brother's was having trouble at home and needed a new place to stay—welcome to our hotel. Suddenly he was in my fucking space and I was not happy.

Fall in central New York is fucking awesome. But soon it ended and the cold and snow were back. My sister would be coming home for Thanksgiving, her first time since going away to college. I was glad; in the short time she was gone I learned to need her a little less and the world a little more. My sister is a big-city person, and being close to Boston was more her style.

My sister brought home a boyfriend, who was relatively nice. It was our first Thanksgiving since Bruce had died, which was a little weird. It was nice to have a holiday in which there was no turmoil or worrying about what would crash down next.

In eighth grade, I made a bunch of new friends that would be the backbone of the next few years and decades of my life. Chris was from the south side of town. Both his parents taught in the public school system and his grandmother lived about a fifteen-minute walk from me. He is a short smartass and I took a liking to him almost immediately. I knew Steve from playing basketball at JP's house; he lived three streets over. He was the good-looking one of the bunch. He also worked the hardest in school out of all of us.

Bob and Nick both came from the same private school. Bob's mom taught English and he was known at this time for his white socks and penny loafers. Nick was tall and goofy—like Kramer on *Seinfeld*. He was loud, like me, and was known for never ever wearing jeans.

Dave, I met the second half of eighth grade—he transferred in late. Dave is a really funny person and very bright; he knows more about the Mets than the Mets know about the Mets. I really got to know him when Chris, Dave, and I played lacrosse, which is also how we met Jamie. Jamie lived around the corner from me and Dan. He was one hell of a competitor, and he would go on and play Division I college lacrosse.

As the holidays passed, these new friends gave me space to be who I needed to be at the time. Playing lacrosse was great, I picked it up easily, lots of running. I really enjoyed being with Chris, Dave, and Jamie on the field. The combination of friends and sport would be a very positive, potent mix for me in the years to come.

I also started to make friends with girls at school. I love my male friends dearly, but sometimes you need a softer conversation, a change of pace. Women, in my experience, provide more empathy and sympathy than men. In high school, when Bob said, "Pete, can you please pass a beer," the word "please" made me flush and sent a tingle down my leg—but sometimes I needed more.

Around this time, I made friends with these three girls I call the Birds of Euclid, since one of them lived on Euclid. They were, and still are, truly nice and funny. They tended not to bust my chops as much as the guys did, at least not until later in high school.

When school ended, Garrett and I spent a lot of time with the Birds. We went and saw some movies and just hung out. Garrett was beyond miserable after two years at his school. I felt bad for his plight, stuck in that school with no end in sight. Garrett and I went fishing with my dad a few times. My brother got a job working nights. He didn't know what he wanted to do with his life after high school. It was 1984 and all anyone wanted to talk was *1984,* the book.

But for me, for the first time in my life it felt as though things were flowing in my direction. I ended up mowing a few lawns that summer and doing odd jobs. If I wanted money in my pocket, I had to come up with it on my own. I never had an allowance and my parents didn't have money to spend on me going out with my friends. But I had enough steady gigs to keep me busy. My sister spent the summer out of town working, so I wouldn't see her again until Thanksgiving.

My eighth grade school picture. I thought that I was safe because my brother was dead. Unfortunately, the fuse was lit for my destruction. I did not end up in smiles.

High school started in September. I was excited that Dan and I were going to be in the same school again. In fact, pretty much everyone from my class at Our Lady of Solace would now be going to William Nottingham High School.

Dan fit right with the guys. It was great to have such an important part of my support system in school with me again.

Bob, Steve, and I went out for freshman football. It was the first time I had played any organized football, but I had a good time and met a bunch of good guys. I liked going home tired after every practice, and slept great. I needed sports to push me into good night sleeps whenever I could fined them.

A week or so into school Larry showed up like a poor, wet kitten in the rain. He lived up the street from Nick and had been friends with him since birth. Larry went to the same school as Nick and Bob, but was still stuck there for eighth grade.

And then, finally, Garrett ended up at Nottingham. He must have threatened his parents with some pretty heavy shit. He was so happy to be there—like a whole different person—and I was thrilled to have him with me again. All of the pieces were coming together for the first time in my life.

The first two weeks of school, my group of friends, with a few others, would form my core group of male friends in high school: a mix of the old and the new. I would spend a lot of time for the next four years with these guys. Ninth grade puts you right back at the bottom of the pile, but I got to spend it with them. I now had a place where I felt safe.

Also, Nottingham had very good athletics. We used to go to all the football games, and all the basketball games, to support Dan. We had Division I talent in both basketball and football.

It was a good time to be a local reporter, since Syracuse had lots of good all-around athletic talent. Sometimes we even got local on-air talent to show up and watch. Whether you are writing about it, watching it, or playing it. Syracuse University is known for putting out great talent in the sports broadcasting world.

After football season, I needed a job, now that I was out of cash from the summer and we all had stuff to do on the weekends. Garrett was working part time at a tennis and racquetball club doing maintenance, keeping the place clean, and there was another opening, so I took it. I worked there every day after school, plus one day per weekend. I would walk the two and a half miles after school, and then my mom would pick me up about 6:30 p.m. My dad would drive me on weekends and pick me up.

Everything went back to the way it was before, after Bruce went into the Marines. My parents eventually moved out of their bad space and things returned to normal. They never asked me about who I was and what I did and I never told them. When I was ten or so, my parents had kind of thrown me the keys and asked "You got this?" and that had been the way it was ever since. I never asked what they thought and they never asked me; it was assumed things were good and life was moving on in an orderly fashion. My father took no interest in my extracurricular activities and, though my mom would occasionally come to one of my games, she had a general lack of knowledge of what she was watching. My parents knew I did things, they just made no effort in supporting me.

My sister came home again that Thanksgiving sans boyfriend, but with three women in tow instead. One of them had been kicked out by her dad, a prominent heart surgeon and staunch Catholic that did not allow gays in his house, even if they were his daughter. So, she and her girlfriend came and stayed at our house. Welcome to the scholarship house, kids!

It was a pretty fun weekend, spending time with my sister. My parents really enjoyed the new company and having a full Thanksgiving table.

Coming up on Christmas, everything was still going pretty fine. I was working after school and hanging out with friends on weekends. Like a lot of kids of the time, we went to high school parties, drank beer, and smoked cigarettes. Also, Larry and I found that we both shared an affinity for smoking pot. I liked the buzz it provided, but I didn't really understand the internal mechanisms it was soothing until later.

My sister came home for Christmas, with no one in tow this time. I think my parents may have been a little disappointed. It was a quiet Christmas, just us and my grandmother. It was this holiday I found out my sister's secret fight against my grandmother's shit-talking: three fingers of bourbon instead of one. I watched in amazement as this experiment was carried out right before my eyes. Get three shots of bourbon into my grandmother and she shuts the fuck up! My grandmother seemed to speak a little less, and perhaps listen a little more.

In spring, I joined the freshman lacrosse team with Chris—we played lacrosse together for all of our high school years. I always got the same feeling after playing lacrosse that I did when I ran the half-mile—a great freedom. I moved to just working weekends, both Saturday and Sunday.

We also started to hang out more. Chris would stay up at his grandmother's house and we would go to an early movie on Westcott Street and then head to a keg party at the Towers, or the field behind Nottingham. I finally felt like my peers, on their level and heading in the same direction. I was beginning to enjoy life.

Spring also brought a big family surprise. One night I was hanging out in my room when my brother showed up.

"Hey, got a sec?" my brother asked.

"Yeah, what's up?" I replied.

He grew quiet for a second, searching for the right words. "I'm thinking about going into the Marines," he said then. He was not joking.

"Whoa, really? Do Mom and Dad know?" I whispered back.

"No. I am about to tell them right now," he said.

"Okay, well, good luck with that."

I looked at him for a second and he turned around and

went into the living room. I turned up the radio.

After about an hour, I heard him go upstairs. I gave it a few minutes, knowing my parents were probably talking about him, then went out to the living room. My mom was visibly upset, blowing her nose. My dad looked pensive, with his hands folded across his mouth. My mom looked at me and asked if I knew and I said I did. I told her it would be okay and that he would be okay. She said she knew, but I could tell she was frightened.

I went up to my brother's room. "How did they take it" I asked.

"Not as bad as I thought. Mom cried and Dad was quiet. I told them why I wanted to do it and they seemed okay with it."

I looked at him. It was a ballsy call and even more so to tell my parents. "I support you, kid," I said and gave him a wink.

I was still hanging out with the Birds of Euclid. They were fun to hang out with but the more I did, the more it scared me. These three bright women had empathy, and were nice and curious—traits you would think would be nice to have in a female friend. But those traits were very dangerous to me and I wouldn't really understand why for some years. They provided a clear and present danger to anyone trying to keep a secret, especially my secret. You hang out, drink a beer, share a cigarette, engage in simple conversation that soon becomes dangerous. I learned to hone an unconscious skill: keeping smart, empathetic women at bay.

The summer started with some excitement: old friends, new friends, and smoking pot with Larry. I also got a new job working in a florist shop. I would sweep up around the shop and greenhouse, move stock, receive plant and flower shipments. During the summer I worked around five days a week, which was decent money.

My dad's brother came to visit right after July 4th for a couple of days. He and my dad were going out on the Saturday and he persuaded me to come, because I am an idiot. They were going to run some errands and then stop and see the firemen competition at Onondaga Lake Park. Let's just say, I never went anywhere with my uncle and father again.

The summer went along with no more family incidents. I spent time with the Birds and the guys. I liked the new job. But again, I felt my life get another very thin film placed over it —everything again got just a little bit more confusing: conversations, work, schoolwork, everything. It took more of an effort just to be normal.

This seemed to have nothing to do with Bruce. As a matter of fact, his abuse was something I rarely thought about. My mind was busy trying to keep me thinking about everything and anything, except what I was doing. I felt like a tire with a little less air, moving from side to side and not able to get enough speed. My brother spent the summer working with my dad, training for the Marines.

We headed into sophomore year knowing we were not freshman anymore. A couple weeks into the school year, my brother was off to Parris Island and basic training. My parents took him to the bus station for his trip. My mom cried a lot, after.

It was the first time in my life that I was alone in the house, truly alone. My siblings were all gone. I wandered around the house and listened to the silence; the house was all mine now. I sat and thought about all the things that had happened in the house over the last couple of years. After about ten minutes I went to Dan's. Some things never change.

I was working in the florist shop a couple days after school and usually one day a weekend—more if business warranted it. In October, a good female friend of mine, LG, got a job there. It was great to have someone I knew from school to talk to. Another classmate and friend of LG's, AT, also got a job there, and LG's mom also worked there on weekends sometimes. What ended up being a part-time job to make money turned into a fun time with friends.

Sophomore year, we all started to learn to drive and our reach expanded. In the spring, we started to play basketball at

Tecumseh Middle School in Dewitt, right across the Syracuse border. If we were not in another sport season, and it was good weather outside, that's where you could find us. It was a small court that fit four on four perfectly. By the time we showed up after school, the middle-school kids and teachers had cleared out, so we had the place to ourselves.

The summer of tenth grade, most everyone had jobs, or was off to a sports camp for a week, but whoever was available would meet around 5 p.m. and play basketball. Then we would go home, eat, shower, and decide what to do that night: beers at the field, movies, laser tag at Jamie's house, or just hanging out. We were our own best amusement.

My sleep was erratic. I sometimes woke up in the middle of the night with my mind running as if I was in a conversation.

Junior year started and we were now upperclassman, woohoo. This was the year that my mind started to tell me that certain situations were untrue.

In the fall, we all went out on a Friday night. A bunch of us guys were out and about, just chatting it up like always. In the process, I got my wires crossed in a conversation and thought I had pissed off Steve something fierce. My brain misread how Steve was acting and attributed his response to me and my actions and words; it was telling me he was angry and I needed to be careful. I spent the rest of the night avoiding him. It was the first time my brain was telling me that something was real, when it was not.

The next day at work I was spinning, wondering what I did wrong. That night, I made sure to stand on the other side of the group, so as not to escalate anything. The night was normal, we busted each other's balls and then said good night.

That night, I was up until about 4 a.m. obsessing, tracing back all the conversations of that evening. But I could not come up with what went wrong. All day Sunday, I wound myself around this.

The next day at school, I was at my locker in the morning and a couple guys stopped by; we chatted while I put my stuff away. Then, suddenly, Steve was standing right there and I didn't say a word. There were some hellos and a few pleasantly exchanged "fuck offs" and the obligatory daps. The bell rang and people dispersed. I had my books and I was closing my locker. People said their goodbyes and Steve looked at me and said "See you later, Pedro," his usual nickname for me, and he wandered off to class with a smile on his face.

This would become a common theme with my friends: the more I hung out with someone, the more my brain would begin to misperceive or misinterpret our interactions. My brain would construe them negatively, and take me on these mental rides, making me think I did or said something wrong. I would stay up at night, or my daily thoughts would be consumed by them. My brain would spin like a broken, warped car tire; with no brakes or direction. I didn't know how to stop any of this, so I just swallowed it. It all sat on a baseline of elevated fight or flight, which had been brewing for years; with no way to turn it off, it just stewed. Before this, anxiety and fear were just general feelings. Now they had form.

In the spring, I played lacrosse as usual, but varsity now. Around the third or fourth game, we were playing some team out of league. I was playing midfield and the ball was on the ground. I couldn't get to the ball without committing a few penalties—not that I am opposed to that. I got a knee in my throat, and thought I heard an opposing player say the name "Bruce" as he picked up the groundball.

I started to freak out a little. Playing defense on the closest pair of shorts I didn't recognize, not even sure if they had the ball or we did. We went down and I was shadowing my man. Play stopped, there was a horn to change players, and my midfield line went off.

I didn't even take my helmet off—just walked to the end of

the bench, grabbed a cup and just started pouring water through my face mask, straight into my mouth. One of the guys was looking at me do this and he must have wondered what was up. The rest of the game, I made no move to play offense—I didn't trust myself to. Something was going on and I didn't want to have the ball and then start to freak out again.

After the game, when most of the equipment was put away, I bolted and went home, straight to my room, and shut the door. I sat on my bed and tried to figure out what happened. I had heard that name a thousand times, from my mom to my dad—but now, I felt like I'd been beat up, I was so tense. It really fucked with my mind, a weird invasion of my mental space. Frightening, almost like a warning.

Junior year was the year I learned what true sadness was. That September I found out my dad's cousin, who was a priest, was gravely ill. He was also gay, had been diagnosed with AIDS that August, and was now in the hospital, waiting for his last days to end. My sister was back and forth, in and out of town to check on him. She and Eddy were tight before the diagnosis and even tighter now.

Back in those days, without any therapeutics, or cures, AIDS patients just withered away, hollowing out until there was nothing left to support their vital organs. It took weeks, months, and all you could do was love and support them, because there was no reprieve.

I went to visit him a few times with my mom, and it was totally gut-wrenching. One of the last times I was there, he was trying to give my mom instructions about his parishioners: "Mrs. Jones does not get out much, so please make sure you stop in and check on her, here's the address. Oh, and Mrs. Vitelli is having a hard time with her son, so check with her and see if things have changed, you may need to sit with him and see what is wrong." Here was a man knowing he was going to die, and all he could think about was what others needed.

Each time I went to see him, Eddy was smaller and smaller —sinking into himself, almost floating on the hospital bed. The last time I saw him, about mid-October, he probably only weighed 110 pounds, if that. His face was so gaunt, I didn't recognize him. He didn't have the strength, or muscle mass, to crack his always-present, infectious smile. But at least he was at peace with his circumstances, which made it a little easier on us.

And then we learned that he had died, and that the bishop of his county had forbidden any priest to attend the funeral because he died of "that disease and lived that way." My family was a little pissed about that. My sister was coming for the funeral.

My mom was with my grandmother, who was still oblivious as to what had happened to Eddy. (My grandmother had a couple friends that were gay. In those days you could live together and you were just called spinsters and nobody ever saw your bedroom on the second floor of your house. My sister kind of relished telling my grandma about her friends, busting her preconceived notions about gay people; they are friendly, good card players, and good friends.) My sister and I walked into the church locked in arms, our usual funeral procession, so the other could not run. We got a few steps in and just stopped—in the crowd were about 100 to 150 priests, all defying the bishop's decree. *Fuck yeah! Fuck that bishop!*

Cousin Eddy was the most compassionate and decent person I have ever met. In his death, he expressed the need to tend to his flock, even when he didn't have the strength to breathe. This world could use a lot more Cousin Eddies.

In the spring, Garrett and Bob and I were over at Jamie's playing basketball one day when his parents happened to be having a party. We were playing-two-on-two and Garrett got the rebound, swinging his arms like an unhinged animal seeking to destroy all in his path. His elbow popped me in my right cheekbone, right below the eye where the skin is thin.

Suddenly everyone was looking at me. I just looked back at

them and said "What?"

Jamie looked at me and pointed to his right eye. I looked down and something was dripping from my face. I reached up to my eye and pulled my finger away with blood on it.

We stopped playing and walked over to the deck, where the adults were hanging out. As Jamie's mom saw me, she hollered for her husband. I was brought over to a chair and sat down.

Jamie's dad came over, a super nice guy who used to be a linebacker for Syracuse University and played with Floyd Little. He looked me over and complimented me on my boxer's cut. He looked me over for a second and said he'd be right back.

Jamie's dad put a tray down with some stuff on it. He picked up a piece of gauze, folded it, doused it in hydrogen peroxide, and placed it over the cut. He then took an ice cube and placed it on the gauze and instructed me to hold it there. He said I should go to the hospital and I told him my parents were out of town. Adults kept coming by and looking and I just gave my English royal hand wave.

Jamie's dad patted the area dry, took out a small butterfly band aid and put it over the cut. He then opened another, pinched my skin just a touch and put the other one on.

The next day, Garrett's mom, who was a nurse, came by at my mother's request and looked at the cut and commented it was closed very nicely. She also mentioned to my mom that I needed a tetanus shot.

The next day I missed lacrosse practice to go get the shot. I had a huge lump on my arm from the shot and it was on fucking fire. Later that night my dad called me over to his chair, grabbed my arm, and quickly swung his other hand down on the lump, pressed, and turned. It hurt like hell while he was doing it, but when he was done it felt a lot better. My father got a tetanus shot when he was a kid and had such a bad reaction he was in a sling for three days. He told me his father had rubbed out the muscle in much the same way. That was the only real father-son generational thing my father ever really did with me.

Junior year ended with people talking about going to college and picking out majors. I remember realizing that the last years of my life, all I had subconsciously been thinking about was being safe. I had not been thinking about a career or college. I never had any dreams about being something when I grew up. I didn't even know if tomorrow was going to happen—I had spent so much time thinking it wouldn't that the concept of needing to plan for it was foreign. I just wanted to be safe, and to feel safe. It was what my brain was trained to do, from the day long ago when Bruce had abused me.

Just one more mornin'
I had to wake up with the blues
Pulled myself out of bed, yeah
Put on my walkin' shoes
And went up on the mountain
To see what I could see
The whole world was fallin',
Right down in front of me.[8]

CHAPTER 12

My brother reached out to my parents and checked in with letters, giving the basics of his Marine life. He had lost 60 percent of his hearing in one of his ears and the Marine doctors didn't know why. My dad was a little livid and wanted to know what was going on.

The Sergeant Major of the Marine Corps is a unique rank; there's only one, and they serve a four-year term. That spring, Sergeant Major of the Marine Corps Harold G. Overstreet got the chance to meet my dad on a phone call.

I came home from school that day and saw my dad's car, which was unusual. I walked in the front door and he came out of the kitchen with a small grin on his face.

I stopped and looked up at him. "What's up, why are you home?"

"I just got off the phone with the Sergeant Major of the Marine Corps," he said as his smile widened. "I told him your brother had problems with his ear and I'd had a son in Beirut and I wanted answers, damn it."

I just stared at my dad, wondering if he could sense my sheer panic. For the next two weeks, every time a car door slammed, I expected a Marine SWAT team to come bursting through the door and drag my dad off.

Luckily, they'd found an earwax buildup in my brother's ear, and once it was cleared out he was fine and back to blowing the shit out of stuff.

Senior year, I quit my florist job and was on the hunt for a new one. The local pharmacy was hiring, and I was hired. It was cool because a few people in my class worked there also; we had a lot of fun. At times there would be just a manager and three or four of us from school, closing up the place.

I applied and got accepted to Niagara University in Niagara Falls, New York. I was a political science major for no other reason than it seemed like I'd like it. I was going to college because my friends were going to college; I really had no idea what I wanted to do. The thought was very abstract to me. I didn't get choices; I was given paths and a push. Mostly, I just didn't want to be left behind.

My dad and mom never sat down and talked with me about such matters, or anything. I am still waiting for my talk about sex. Now, you may find that funny, but parents are supposed to pass knowledge onto their children and help them. That was not my dad's speed, and my mom never seemed interested. The only talk we ever had about a career was my dad saying "You can grow up and be whatever you want to be." I was going to have to figure this out on my own, again.

It was the end of senior year in April, my brother wrote saying that he was in Subic Bay, Philippines. He would then be sailing around the Sea of Japan and doing some maneuvers.

Then, April 15 hit. No, not taxes: the Tiananmen Square showdown between protesters and the Chinese army. Politicians were discussing intervening and sending Marines, which brought the feeling of anxiety and dread right back to my parents. It poured off them like molten steel and rolled onto me. Feeling it again was horrible, but fortunately no Marine was ever sent. Unfortunately, the protests were met by violence from the Chinese government and thousands were killed and injured. The fear spiked my anxiety something fierce, but I didn't recognize it as such, nor did anyone around me.

The summer of my senior year, I worked overnight in a grocery stocking shelves. It paid better money than the pharmacy. I started at 10 p.m. and went until 6 a.m., Tuesday through Saturday, so I didn't see the guys that much that summer, except for playing basketball. It was hard missing the last summer with them, but in a couple of months I was going away to college and I wouldn't have them as a crutch anymore.

I didn't put together the true mathematics of my relationship with my friends and our activities until years later. Our split and lack of exercise would have a pronounced negative effect on me. That combination was my therapy at the time, so when that disappeared, so did I.

The fall of 1989, I started college in Niagara Falls, New York. Over the summer I definitely felt another layer filling in over me. Ever so slightly, things got more difficult and drawn out. I wanted conversations to end sooner. My fight-or-flight had risen and my patience for people had diminished. I had not had to make new friends since seventh grade.

Over the summer, the school hosted a weekend where we went to get tested for math and English, and I saw my floormate Rob that weekend, which made things easier. He had another few friends, so soon it was a group of about eight of us guys. We lived in a male dorm, so we wouldn't meet the fairer sex until later. I really didn't hang out with my roommate at all. He was a nice guy, but we were just into different things.

I got a job at the school library. Things were moving along: school during the week, parties on the weekend. It was not illegal for us to have beer in our dorm room, as long as it was cans. One of the guys had a real fake ID he got by using someone else's information. Most of us had chalked IDs, which were pretty good to get into the college bars downtown.

College was okay; I missed my friends from home. They had made things so easy. The guys I met at college were good enough guys, from all over the state and a few out-of-staters. One thing is for sure, my drug use grew. Being closer to the Canadian border, we could get access to black hashish and mescaline. Hashish was a new smoke for me and I truly enjoyed it; same with mescaline and LSD. By no means was it a regular thing and I do not condone the use of either.

We would take it and hang out in someone's room, listen to music, or go walking across campus in the shadows. Or we'd go next door to the parking lot of the Niagara Power Vista and go ice-skating at night; during the day, the sun would warm enough to melt snow and the water would refreeze at night, leaving a sheet of ice on the surface. The one thing I remember about taking mescaline or LSD was how clear my mind felt the days after. My body felt like shit the next day, but my mind had a clarity I liked.

There was not much to do at the university in 1989, and if you didn't have a car you were stuck on campus—hello, booze and drugs. We had room parties where people would buy a bunch of cases. Some guys in our dorm actually had a fully stocked bar.

Around the last week of September, Larry came and picked me up to bring me back to Syracuse. I had purchased tickets to the Rolling Stones concert for the 22nd. I also sold a couple of tickets to a few of my college friends and they were going to drive down and stay with my parents after the show.

The show was a great time: Living Colour opened, and they were spectacular. We went out after the show to a bar, then spent the night with my parents and they made us breakfast the next day. We headed back to school on Sunday. It was a nice little trip and gave me a taste of home that I was missing. College was the longest I had spent away from home.

I came home again for Thanksgiving and it was great to see the guys. I didn't realize how much I missed them until I saw them —good things came flooding back, like a warm breeze. I also got to see my sister, who was living in New York City. Her boyfriend had come home with her and he seemed alright.

The last few weeks of the semester went quick. The campus began to empty out as the testing week moved forward. The night before the last test, a snowstorm blew through, all the way to Syracuse. My dad saw the weather forecast and hit the highway as soon as he could. On the way to get me, they declared a state of emergency because of the snow, but he kept coming.

Eventually he pulled into a hotel parking lot in a town between Buffalo and Niagara Falls. He was literally the only car there and he ended up jumping the curb to get in because he could not see the entrance to the parking lot. When he went in and got a room, the guy was amazed to see my dad, since half his rooms had called and cancelled and the other half had not shown up.

When I woke up the next morning, the snow banks were huge—walls of snow. I called my mom to see where my dad was and she told me he had left the night before and would be there to pick me up. After my last test, I walked to the spot where I'd told him I would be and there he was. He sped over to the dorm and I got my bag. The flurries were starting again and we bolted for Syracuse.

Winter break was great, seeing the guys again. We spent pretty much all of our time together: a movie on Christmas Eve, a party here and there, or just hanging out. I really didn't want the break to end, that was for sure. Splitting up again was hard.

I went back to school and another layer was added—an imaginary mental film that just kept getting thicker. I had no control over it. Conversations were harder, because I wanted them to end, no matter who I was talking to and what we were talking about. I was always trying to keep my secret and it just made my life in general more difficult. The more layers, the harder it became to keep it together and act like nothing was wrong. I didn't really know what I was doing there; I didn't know what I wanted to do and felt like I was wasting time. I was comparing my friends at home to my friends at school, which made it so hard to be there.

As the spring semester carried on, I decided I didn't want to come back to school. I felt like all I was doing was treading water. I had no direction and felt that, if I stayed, it would turn into something bad. The whole place just didn't feel right. I had not told my parents yet, but I think they had an idea this was coming. An event at the end of the year sealed it.

I told Nick he should come up to campus and hang out: a Grateful Dead cover band was playing and a whole bunch of parties were happening. He agreed to come up Saturday, and I was excited.

At my library job, my relief on Sunday nights was a kid we'll call Harry, from East Syracuse. I remember him distinctly. Harry would arrive and I would stay and chat a minute or two —very nice kid, with a smile that made you feel at ease. He got a Mickey Mouse tattoo on his calf during spring break, which he was kind enough to show me.

It was the Wednesday before spring break. The weather was great, finally shifting to spring. There was a group of guys on the sixth and eighth floors of our dorm that we called the accounting guys.

Apparently, the sixth-floor dorm phone rang and it was Harry. He was down at the falls and he wanted to jump. One of the accounting guys answered the phone, and told him to hang on; they were coming down and wanted to talk to him. They hung up the phone and moved out.

When the guys got down there, Harry was amped and near the edge. He said he didn't want to go home, it was not a good place. The guys stood there and talked to him for about ten minutes and persuaded him away from the edge. They walked up the sidewalk and told him they would go back to school and come up with a plan. If he didn't want to go home, he wouldn't have to.

They took about five more steps, but then suddenly Harry turned on his heel and, in a full sprint, ran down the sidewalk and jumped into the falls, using a bench as a springboard. In a second he was gone—he slipped away from view and into the falls. His body was never recovered.

I ran into these guys after they pulled into the parking lot after talking to the police. They got out of the car and you could tell in a second something was dreadfully wrong. I went over and they were upset. As they relayed the story to me I just stood there, completely fucking dumbfounded.

I sat down and my friend who had been at the falls sat next me and started hysterically crying. He fell over into my lap and I put my head on his shoulder and I started to cry. I had no words for him; I could not think of one thing to say that would comfort him. I do not know how long we were there, it felt like hours, but the sun was still up and not getting hazy yet. The air of the university just deflated. The spring break everyone was saving up for became a spring wake.

I called Nick, upset, that Thursday night. I could not get Harry out of my mind. Nick ended up coming Saturday night.

On Tuesday we had a meeting in the library to discuss Harry; it was hard as fuck reliving that again. I ended up taking a couple of his shifts the last few weeks of school. I wished I had gotten to know him more, but then it would have been even harder. I found out from his girlfriend that things at home were actually dangerous. Home is not supposed to be dangerous; it is supposed to be a happy, safe, and healing place.

School ended and I was not coming back. Harry's suicide was the icing on the cake. Having no direction and after the tragedy befalling this poor kid, I just could not see myself going through the motions anymore. I told my parents when I got home and they seemed fine with it.

And so the summer of 1990 began, and "The bus came by and I got on, that's when it all began, there was Cowboy Neal at the wheel of the bus, to never ever land."[9]

It was nice to be home again and it was really nice to see the guys. I'd made it a whole school year without them. I got a job busing tables at a local Mexican restaurant. It was a busy place and I made good money. But on July 16, 1990, the best thing that ever could happen, happened.

I got Grateful Dead tickets for the Buffalo show at Rich

Stadium and asked who wanted to go. Nick and Chris were in, and FW said he would drive. We left Syracuse that day about 2 p.m., which was a mistake. We should have left the night before, or very early in the morning. The party started way before we showed up and it was rocking when we rolled in, raging without us.

Balloons, kites, frisbees—the sky was full of flying fun. Flags were waving everywhere and you could borrow a cup of cheer from almost anyone. I had already taken a hit of LSD, which just made everything pop. I was ready to get inside and experience my very first Grateful Dead show.

It was fucking magic. This was my kind of place and these were my kind of people. I enjoyed every second of that day and that show. It took me to a new place and I have been on the bus ever since. *Not fade away...*

The rest of the summer I was just trying to figure out a next move. I was unsure what I wanted to do with my life. I had been left to figure out things by myself, so the idea of asking for help was foreign to me. When you eat dinner across the table from your abuser for years, a day has more to do with the sun rising, than with thinking about tomorrow's options. I learned not to dream at a young age, so dreaming about what I wanted to be when I grew up didn't happen. My brain was wired differently than that, but at the time I didn't know it.

Sophomore year, TC and Larry lived in a dorm up on Mount Olympus. Nick was living down on the south side of town, going to the local community college, and Jamie and Dave were in a south campus apartment living with the Syracuse University athletes. Everyone else was at school out of town.

I spent a lot of time with Dave and Jamie at their apartment when I was not working. I tried going back to school again, and it just did not work. I wanted to take culinary classes because it was something that I was interested in.

I was also thinking of joining the Marines. You may be a

little amazed to hear that. But if there was one thing I knew I needed in my life, other than tickets to the summer Dead tour, it was a little discipline. I needed a way to find out what I wanted to do.

Sometimes I would go to SU basketball games with Jamie and Dave, but it sucked because I had to sit by myself. They got their tickets, but they were in the student/athlete section, which I could not access. So, sometimes on game night if we were going to hang out, they would go to the game and I would hang at their apartment until they returned. On January 16, 1991, Syracuse University was playing the University of Connecticut in the Carrier Dome.

We beat Connecticut by two points—a really good game, right down to the buzzer. Jamie, Dave, and AB came barreling in and I stood up off the couch and said, "Good game" and AB looked up at me.

"We just bombed Iraq. They announced it over the PA system at the game."

I was dumbfounded; I just stood there for a second and said nothing. We turned on the news and watched our military just bomb away. I walked out the back sliding door of their apartment and lit a cigarette. I thought about me joining the Marine Corps and the sound of my mother wailing when Bruce died came into my head. I could not do this to my parents; I put the thought away.

The summer of 1992, I got an apartment with Larry and our friend Peter, and two other guys that Peter knew from school. The five of us rented an apartment on Harrison Street, the same street as Salt City Theater.

It was good to get out of my parents' house. I enjoyed living with the guys, especially Peter and Larry. I got a job cooking at a pub that Peter worked at on the Syracuse campus, six days a week. I enjoyed the freedom to just be myself. I was busy working and the guys went to school. They all worked either in the pub I worked at, or across the street at a different bar. It was good to go out to the bars and hang out with people my own age, even though I was not going to school.

The following year, Larry went and roomed with the two guys that we lived with and Peter and I lived together with two girls. The five-guy house had been a little too much testosterone. It was nice to have the ladies soften the joint up, plus they smoked pot too. I moved up to waiting tables at the pub and some bar-backing. But I was dealing with another layer and it made a good time much harder.

Garrett and Bob, along with a friend of Bob's, AS, got an apartment together. Garrett was working at a bar downtown before he went off to law school and Bob was getting ready to start graduate school to become a teacher.

Before Christmas, I got the news that Garrett's mom was sick with cancer. I was thrown for a loop. She was in her midforties and my mom's best friend. It wasn't serious yet, but my mom still worried and Christmas was a little dark that year. Midwinter, she was diagnosed stage 4.

One day in spring, I was home during the day and the phone rang. It almost never rang during the day because everyone was at class, except me. I picked up the phone and said hello.

"Hi, Pete?" the voice said on the other line.

I knew it was my father and I knew she was dead. "She's dead, huh?" I asked rather solemnly.

"Yeah, about an hour ago or so. I don't have any details yet."

We both sat there quietly for a second. He told me he would be back in touch with the details later. I told him I had to work that night at the pub and he said he would call before I left.

I hung up the phone and sat down and cried. I felt so bad for Garrett. I made a few phone calls and once my dad called back with details about everything, I reached out to the guys about a plan.

I went to the wake with a couple of the guys. I walked in, saw a few people, and paid my respects. Then, I could hear my mom. She sounded pretty distraught and I went to her and consoled her for a bit. She was crushed.

I made my way over to Garrett, his dad, and his sister, and paid my respects. I was so hurt for them; it was just the fucking worst. I hung out for a while with my parents and then made my way back to the guys.

I didn't have to work the night before the funeral and I went out drinking. I was drinking a lot then and smoking too many cigarettes. We ended up staying up the whole night and I didn't end up leaving the pub with Larry and Peter until about 5 a.m. There was no sense in sleeping because I would have to get up in a few hours anyway. We went to the funeral and sat in the back.

We spent the day over at Garrett's and Bob's place hanging out, then went to the pub and got some food. We had not really eaten all day, but we had consumed a shitload of beer. We hung out there for a few hours and drank.

I thought about the times I'd spent with his mom. She took us whitewater rafting once. All the times I'd slept over at his house. All the rules we so desperately tried to break. All of those thoughts just became final memories. You never know when you will have your last memory of someone.

The following summer I moved back home. Although I was seeing friends, going out and being social, I just did not feel right. It felt as though everything was a trillionth of a second off. I felt like I could not give people my undivided attention.

My mom was all over the place. She was pretty despondent after the funeral, which I understood. I did some thinking and decided I wanted to go to culinary school and was thinking of moving to New Orleans. I ran the idea by Nick and since he was done with school, he said he would come along.

I was bartending and waiting tables at the pub—good money. Nick and I decided that we would move after the New Year. I knew a guy, RC, who was moving down to New Orleans and we would touch base with him when we arrived.

Nick and I packed up our things and rented a truck and took off in mid-January. We drove our U-Haul right to RC's house. He lived right around the corner from one of the best bars in the world, the Maple Leaf Bar.

We lived with RC for about two weeks before we found a place on Magazine Street. New Orleans is not the place to keep your liver or waist in a safe state, but it sure is fun. I got a job waiting tables at this restaurant in the mall in the French Quarter and it was horrible. The owner sucked, the staff sucked, and the patrons were horrible. It was just a bad-vibe place. Nick got a job waiting tables while he was looking for acting work.

I ended up getting a much better job at an Italian fine dining restaurant owned by a guy who actually went to my brother's high school, after he emigrated from Calabria. He also knew Junior, the owner of our favorite pizza shop, Johnny's, back in Syracuse. It was a great job making good money. It also turned me on to real home-cooked Italian food. My mother was a jar sauce woman.

I liked living in New Orleans. The food was great and the music was unbelievable. You could walk into any bar uptown and hear some world-famous musician play for free and then hang out in the crowd and drink a beer. Nick and I went out to watch the Super Bowl at a bar called Madigan's and ended up in a conversation with guitarist Camile Baudoin, from the Radiators, for a couple hours. That was just a typical night in New Orleans.

In the fall of 1996, I got a phone call from my mom. She did not sound good. I was worried about her, not only because she got diagnosed with breast cancer and would end up getting a mastectomy, but because both my parents have a habit of keeping bad health results from their children. This lack of communication would be an ongoing concern.

I was so worried that, much to Nick's chagrin, I made plans to move home and be with my mom. That early December

I packed up my things and moved back to Syracuse. When I was in New Orleans I had realized something was wrong with me, but I didn't know what.

It was snowing in Syracuse when I got back. My mom and dad were glad to see me. I got my old job doing some bartending back at the pub and also worked a night across the street at another bar.

Around this time, my relationship with my dad started to thaw a little. We had watched football on Sundays for four years during high school and barely said a word. He was just not built to interact with a teenager.

CHAPTER 13

Spring was ending and I still didn't have any idea what I was going to do. My friend HW was having a party and invited me over. A bunch of people from the Syracuse University bar scene were there, plus neighbors and other friends.

A bunch of us were hanging in a circle, just talking. HW looked over at this gentleman RH, a concert stage manager. "Hey, do we need any climbers for next week?"

"Of course we do. Him?" RH responded, while pointing at me and smiling.

HW looked at me and asked, "What are you doing this summer? You want to go to Washington, DC, next week and build a stage for a rock festival?"

That Wednesday I was on my way to Washington to build a stage for my first rock show. They were going to pay me to watch music! My first show consisted of Presidents of the United States, Foo Fighters, Cracker, Fred Schneider, No Doubt, Garbage, Dishwalla, and Girls Against Boys, to name just a few.

I loved the job; it was outside, good hard labor. The days were long and hot, with intermittent rain. I helped build the stage and then I got to work the day of the show. After the show, it took us the entire next day to get the stage out.

I returned to Syracuse to do my second show in the Syracuse Carrier Dome, for Promise Keepers, an evangelical group for men. I have never seen so many men in one place with no beer. It was a good gig, took us about a week.

I spent the summer on the road with two guys I'd met, BC and ST. They were both from Vermont and knew each other well, and showed me the ropes.

That first summer, I traveled up and down the Eastern

Seaboard building stages, including a couple of Lollapalooza shows. The 1996 lineup was Metallica, the Ramones, Rancid, Wu-Tang Clan, Violent Femmes, Shaolin Monks, and Soul Coughing, to name a few.

I finished out the summer building the stage for the Great New York State Fair, which I was able to work while sleeping in my own bed at night.

I would go back and work at the pub at Syracuse University during the school year. I had two jobs making good money, but I could not stand myself. I was beginning to hollow out but put up a front at work as best I could. The more I tried to make myself happy, the more I drank. My life was beginning to speed by me and I was not even noticing. I was also not calling friends back, or reaching out like I had in the past—a slow game of self-isolation.

The next year, 1997, was the same: shows scattered and in between I would work at the bar. I either lived with my parents or rented a place, floating back and forth. I also had a dog. No matter where I was, I just felt like I was faking everything, except drinking. Drinking I was doing really well. At the time, I could not understand why I was making money, doing a job I loved, but was so unhappy.

As much as I tried to surround myself with happy, positive people, it didn't rub off. At night, when I was alone, I would sit and spin things in my head: people I had hurt, things not accomplished, places not gone. I would mentally brutalize myself, and when you are drunk, this can be very harrowing at times. I didn't know why I did it. I would lose my job at the pub because of drinking, but I didn't care. My brain didn't want me to care. It pressed me not to show empathy toward myself no matter what. I was losing in a game I didn't recognize I was playing and I had no clue what the rules were.

Summer of '98, I was deteriorating. Dave Matthews and one of my favorite bands, Phish, played in August. Dave's show went off without a hitch. The Phish show was a little different.

While the shows were going on, or we didn't have anything to do, we usually hung out under the stage. If the weather stayed fine, then me and my partners had an easy day playing Pitch, a card game.

Phish production was up on stage and their crew were putting together the finishing touches before their stage manager's last walk-through of the stage. BB, a friend of mine, came up to me under the stage and said he needed to talk to me. He was standing with Mimi Fishman, mother of Phish drummer, Jon. He told me Ms. Fishman could not go up the stairs, because of her knees.

I looked over at Ms. Fishman, who was using a cane at the time. Despite her not-so-great health, she would go down every year she could and attend these shows, hang until 3 or 4 in the morning talking to the kids, and helping them, and that is just fucking badass.

My picture that was printed by the local newspaper.
I am preparing the sound mix for its roof skin at the
Vernon Downs Phish show. Behind me is the main
stage. The photographer asked me my personal
information, but I had no idea it would be printed.

So, looking at Ms. Fishman, her cane, and the stairs, I said, "We are going to put you on a forklift." I smiled. "Ms. Fishman, would you mind going up on a forklift?"

"Oh sure, of course," she said with a smile.

I walked Ms. Fishman back to upstage center on the ground. Ms. Fishman got on a pallet and JR got in front of her and hooked his climbing belt on either side of her. She looked at JR and he smiled his big goofy smile; she held tight to his arms. It looked like they were slow-dancing fourth-grade style!

I puffed on a cigarette. It occurred to me at about five feet off the ground: if Jon Fishman walks out and sees his mom up there, I have no way to explain it really.

CG popped her gently up on the stage, in between the rails. JR unhooked himself and stepped out of the way to help her off the pallet. She turned to thank them and then walked off with Phish's stage manager.

I got a job across the street from the bar I used to work at, where HW worked and MB used to manage. They were putting on live shows, and wanted my help. I was mentally falling apart but I just didn't care. I was giving everyone else 100 percent, and giving myself nothing. Subconsciously, my brain didn't want me to stop and assess anything in my life. I was just plowing through, going through life on muscle memory.

That fall, my mother was in a car accident. The seatbelt left her bruised across her chest, so she got checked out by her doctor. After further examinations, she was told that the breast cancer was back. Lack of self-checking or regular doctors' visits meant the cancer had progressed to where she needed another mastectomy. My mom was scared and so was my dad. I didn't want my mom to die and knew she would disregard the doctor's orders and keep smoking, with a poor diet and no exercise.

It was a weird time. I was trying not to drown in my own raging mental ocean, excited about my new job, and hoping my mom didn't die of cancer.

But my mom was good as could be after the surgery. My sister came up to be with her during and after. I stayed close that winter too, which was not great for my mental health.

The summer of 1999, Woodstock '99 was happening down the road in Rome, New York. I was third in charge of waste management; my immediate boss was BH, who I had been on the road with for the past two years. I showed up to Woodstock '99 in June and didn't leave until September. It was a long, hot summer and definitely one I will remember forever. And so will the music world, unfortunately.

After Woodstock, I worked for BB and SW back in Syracuse, as a stagehand—a couple gigs a week, enough to keep me busy and off the streets. But it didn't keep me from drinking, or keep me out of my own mind.

That December, I got a call about working a couple of weeks in Washington, DC, for the Millennium Celebration, and supervising the building of the stage and seating on the steps of the Lincoln Memorial. The next day BH and I drove to the Lincoln Memorial, checked in with our boss, and got the lay of the land. We were building a stage about twenty feet off the ground from the top step of the memorial and it stretched about fifteen feet past the stairs. We also needed to build viewing stands (bleachers) for guests to sit in, about thirty feet off the ground.

I was in DC for about ten days. It was cold; it flurried a couple of times and rained. One day it rained all day long, I was soaked five minutes after I got there. That night in the hotel room, cold as shit, I took my boots off and sweatshirt and tee. I tried pulling my jeans off, but I could not get them past my hips.

My skin was pale white, with goose bumps, and wrinkly from being wet all day. I lay on my bed and struggled to get my jeans off. I was rolling and pulling, and just could not get the soaked jeans over my skin. I rolled a few more times and rolled right off the bed, and I could hear BH belly laughing at me from his side of the room. I made him buy first round in the bar. Then we all went home for Christmas for three days.

And then were back at it. We pushed hard to make our day-before–New Year's Eve walk-through complete. Temporary staging and seating has to get certified by all city, and/or town zoning and emergency regulations: inspectors and engineers come by and review blueprints, egress, and emergency exit measurements.

Next I got a gig putting stanchions in the middle on the Lincoln Memorial reflecting pool. I had a team of eight guys and we were to build these triangle stanchions out of the same layered scaffolding we use for building stages, just much smaller pieces. They then had to be placed in the middle of the reflecting pool, a certain distance from the next placed stanchion.

I gathered my crew and told a forklift to gather the marked steel stanchions and bring them to the edge of the pool. I was given a fifty-ton crane to place them.

A couple of guys started building stanchions. I passed off the blueprints and went over to the crane. We finally got it in after about forty-five minutes of road building and driving. Getting two stanchions built and in the pool, centered, took almost three hours—and we had to do this the whole distance of the pool, all the way to the Washington Memorial. I needed a new plan.

I had four of my guys put on water waders and they would carry the stanchions out and measure distance. The rest of the guys built the stanchions: measured out where they should be located in the pool, and lined them up on the edge of the pool to be grabbed.

I stayed with the four-man placement team and had two guys bring the stanchions from the edge to the center of the pool; the other two guys would measure the distance between the previously placed stanchions. Once we got a rhythm down, we began to make speedy progress. We placed the stanchions about fifteen feet apart or so; and the pool is 2,000 feet long, so we had about 150 of these to place.

BH and I didn't have to be to work until 1 a.m. January 1, to remove all the soft goods and weather protection so they didn't end up ripping. It was a very surreal moment in time, the millennium crowd ringing it in. 2000 was here and I could not have cared less. I hated myself and where I was.

Taking everything out took about ten days, racking and packing all the steel onto trucks. Once we got down to the base of the stage, it had to be all hand-carried off the steps, because the quarry to replace the marble doesn't exist anymore so we couldn't chip any of the stairs.

We left Washington, D.C. and I went to my parents' house, where my dog Abita mugged me to say hello and literally knocked me over. My mom looked up at me with a big smile and said hello and Happy New Year. Her smile faded quickly when she saw me and the color in my face.

I fell apart with the flu for the next week. I had never felt that bad. Green is not a good look for me.

After I recovered I did a few gigs here and there. I also spent a lot of time with BB and his roommate SW, who played in local bands and taught bass. I did gigs and was waiting to go back on the road. The bar I worked at doing shows had shut down.

In the middle of March I got a call from RW at the staging company asking if I wanted to go on the road supervising the building of stages for the summer. Hell yes!!! I said that I would and after a few phone calls figuring out specifics, I was going to their headquarters in the beginning of April, where we'd spend a couple days packing our trucks, and then we would head down to Nashville, Tennessee, for nineteen days of rehearsals and the George Strait Country Music Festival Tour. The tour would include Tim McGraw, Lee Ann Womack, Martina McBride, Asleep at the Wheel, and Kenny Chesney, to name a few.

We spent the first few days building the stage from the blueprints, making adjustments as we went, cutting soft goods to fit, measuring out weather protection, and getting the loading dock right. I was on a team of six guys, which would whittle down to five. It was the last leisurely build of the summer.

My last two pieces were two main scrims that were forty by fifty feet, with mirrored pictures of George and his son Bubba (George Strait, Jr.) sitting by a campfire. No matter what, nothing could happen to those pieces. They could not be replaced. They were my babies the whole tour.

I started out very happy with what I was doing but I also felt another layer being added to my load, making me want to isolate. It became harder trying to keep it together. My base fight-or-flight had risen dramatically since I was a kid; but it was still so normal to me, it didn't register as wrong, or dangerous. Simple questions felt like huge weights that needed to be lifted off my shoulders. Everything felt urgent, even if it was not a priority. Even when the boss complimented me on a job well done, I second-guessed everything. I projected a wall of invincibility at all times, even though I was crumbling on the inside. My friends that I didn't shut out probably noticed things were not right, but if they did they kept it to themselves. My idea was not to let anyone see anything.

We did Jacksonville and drove up to Cincinnati, which was going to be a straight-in: we started one hour after the baseball game ended and would go nonstop until production rolled in. The weather was not that bad, but the humidity at night left the steel wet, which is very dangerous. There was a huge brouhaha between the one summer hire and our lead and the summer hire got sent home, which meant I was picking up a lot of slack.

We did the Cincinnati show and drove straight to DC to

do two shows in Landover, where the Redskins play. On May 28, we had the HFS Festival: Rage Against the Machine, Stone Temple Pilots, Godsmack, Cypress Hill, Deftones, and Staind, among others.

We did the HFS Festival, but we kept the loading dock for HFS up, as it was designed to be bigger than George Strait's configuration for the show on June 3. As we were taking down the stage right after at 11 p.m., it started to rain and didn't stop—the longest it ever took me to take down a stage.

You could only move so fast because of slippage and safety reasons, but it was also cold, in the fifties that night, and you can only crack the whip so hard before people walk off on you.

My partner and I relaxed the next day at the hotel and then headed to the airport for our last show in Houston. Houston was a fun show, and then I flew to Utah to join a new tour and crew. The next tour, NSYNC No Strings Attached, had already started and I was joining them in Salt Lake City. When I arrived late in the afternoon, a bunch of the stage had already been built, in Rice-Eccles Stadium. We built until about 8 p.m. because a wind storm rolled in that evening.

The next day we started anew and it was a great day. The sun was shining and it was about 80 degrees out with a breeze —perfect building weather. This stage was different from other stages I had built. Instead of the stage height being five or six feet off the ground, this stage was not even a foot high. NSYNC built staging equipment for their band on top of our stage.

I was walking downstage and had just lit a cigarette, admiring the nice day, when I heard a thud—two sprinklers blasting into decks that were a little uneven. Within about ten seconds the stage, along within whoever was within ten feet of it, was drenched. I just stood at the front of the stage, getting soaked, smoking as I formulated a plan. The cacophony of fucks being yelled was quite amusing, except the Mormon administration that heard it was not amused and a reprimand was sent down.

I just stood there and smoked my cigarette. It sure was

a nice day out. I had brought extra socks—I always had a full change of clothes for such special occasions. The sprinklers shut off about a minute later and I turned and looked at everything behind me: the stage was dripping wet, along with everything on it. People popped up from where they had dived for cover. I walked out to the parking lot to ZS's truck, got in to change into my dry clothes, and hung my wet ones out. It was still a very nice day out. ZS was one of my bosses and my lead boss for this tour.

At one point during this show, a colleague took out his decibel meter to get a reading: the crowd was louder than the band at 116db.

Off to Joliet, Illinois!! We took off early the next morning. We would be building the stage on the drag strip in between the jersey barricades. It was a tight fit and kind of an odd place because the nearest tree seemed like it was a mile away. Great weather for the build, though, sunny and mild.

It went smoothly. We had finished everything up by about 5 p.m. and PS had gotten the roof in the air to height, which meant we wouldn't have to fuck with it in the morning while production rolled in. The climbers and I got out of the air, and I found out dinner was ready to go in catering, so I started to walk over to the tent, about fifty yards from the back of the stage. The wind had a chill to it.

In the catering tent there were about ten people eating and another few in line. I got behind RH, a friend from Syracuse who was working production for the tour. As I was grabbing food and chatting, a big gust of wind came in and blew napkins everywhere, knocked a few chairs over, along with the catering sign. It was messy but fine.

I put baked chicken on my plate and grabbed the spoon for the rice. I took two steps and a big gust of wind came in, lifted the tent about two feet off the ground, and slammed it back down.

I bolted out the same entrance, looked left, and saw the sky above the stage was black, with hints of green and blue. Another big gust of wind came through. I was still holding my plate (never take food from a stagehand; you will not get the hand back) of food as I ran from the catering tent. As we were running, RH dropped his plate and grabbed his walkie-talkie with one hand and with his other grabbed the hand mic to secure it as we ran. (Radios are $1,000 a pop.) I was still holding my plate and running, when my rice blasted off my plate like it had been vacuumed up.

The wind temperature had dropped considerably and it looked like it was 9 p.m. I dropped my plate (poor chicken) and hauled ass for another thirty feet, then dropped to the ground. This weird noise started coming from the stage and the roof was starting to flutter, the wind ripping through the stage making this low-range humming.

Then it all happened at once: a microburst (confirmed later by weather officials) blew and picked the roof up about ten feet in the air, where it stayed suspended for about a second or two and then slammed back down. The towers twisted in seconds and you could hear the breaking and bending of a large amount of steel. I could hear the scrims and weather protections being torn apart.

I watched in disbelief as a stage with a width of about 114 feet, a depth of fifty feet, and a height of about sixty feet—totaling about 100,000 pounds of steel and deck—was made into a fourteen-foot-high junkyard. We laid there for a minute and surveyed what was in front of us. Catering was still standing, barely, chairs and tables were scattered. The stage was down, but I didn't know about the mix. I had no idea where ZS or PS were and no idea where the rest of the team was. Fuck!

I got up when I saw the nasty cloud was passing on. There were a few light sprinkles of rain and I could feel large bubbles of cool and warm air passing through. The barometric pressure was screwy, and you could feel it. I didn't like being in this open field, started running toward the stage. As I encountered stagehands and their supervisor, I told them to go under the bleachers, wait, and start a head count.

It was chaos under the bleachers. Stagehands were freak-ing out and there was still not a final head count yet. The local man in charge of the production on the raceway side came over and we huddled, decided we needed to execute a dead walk.

The head of the stagehands said all his people were accounted for. Our group walked out from under the bleachers toward the stage. I looked up and saw the mix (where the sound and light boards in the crowd are used during shows) for the first time. It had been picked up, thrown over the three-foot-high jersey barricade, and tossed about twenty feet, and was now just a pile of steel, tarps, and broken decks. The sixty-foot-high stage was now fourteen feet high and had been knocked off center by a few degrees.

And there in front of us was an eight-foot catering table with three orange Igloo water coolers. The coolers were still on the table, off-center from the wind, but still full and intact. We all just looked at it in amazement. How the fuck did this table not get hit, between the mix and the stage? Surreal and spooky, with the cold clouds above and the devastation on the ground. The wavering barometric pressure gave everything an uneasy feeling.

We broke off into two groups, one going to the left and walking around the stage in the front and my team walking around to the right. We looked into the steel for any signs of people or blood. Once we got to the back of the stage, PS and I looked at each other.

I took my radio off and gave it to ZS to hold. I took my knife out and clipped it to the top of my T-shirt. PS looked at me and asked if I was ready and I nodded. I told ZS if there were any problems, PS would radio out. PS and I looked at each other and started our way into the steel. It was wet, so we had to move slowly and precisely; sliding and falling decks could bash your head open. After about ten minutes we determined that no one was in the steel.

We gathered together to talk about next steps. The show was obviously cancelled. We were going to have to come in the next day and physically tear this stage apart. We spent the day cutting and tearing the stage apart and putting it on to flatbeds to be sold for scrap.

CHAPTER 14

After Illinois, we got sidetracked to do another gig and then I went back to DC to do the NSYNC show in RFK stadium, where I've done more shows than any other venue. It was an easy load-in, typical rainy and humid day in DC.

The show ended and the lights went up. The stadium was clear of patrons so it was just production and stagehands. As I was walking toward the stage I heard a horrendous bang and screams from behind me. I quickly turned around and the climbers who were standing at the back of the mix, up in the spotlight position, were not there—and neither was the deck. I ran toward the mix and that's when I saw two people on the deck of the mix, rolling around, screaming. Lots of screaming.

I sprinted to the mix as fast as I could. There was a single deck and two people on it writhing in pain. One woman was holding her stomach, her face scrunched like a fist, moaning in pain. The other, a male with a huge laceration to his head, seemed very out of it.

I ripped off my T-shirt and put it over the guy's busted-open head—it quickly turned red. I yelled up at a climber to get me a clean towel, and asked another to run and get the EMTs. Two other climbers, I told to rip open the barricade from behind the mix, so the EMTs could get there. I looked down and my T-shirt was really red—I was beginning to freak out a little. I was holding this guy's brain in and I did not want him to die. He didn't want to die. It was the first time I had ever asked myself that someone not die.

I looked up and saw an EMT running toward us. She was short and a little round and I was wondering how she was going to get up to us; we were about four feet off the ground and she had a big gig bag of EMT gear slung over one shoulder. I saw her make a wide turn, pick up speed, and start sprinting right at me. And then she fucking stage-dove right up toward me, like a dark-blue Superwoman, with those funny scissors in her pant-leg pocket—sliding right across her boobs and popping up to her knees next to me.

She ripped open her bag and barked at me to get "that disgusting T-shirt off his head." I did, and saw that the cut was huge—I could see his skull. She quickly pressed a sterile bandage on his head, told me to cut off both his and the woman's shoelaces. I took out my knife, cut the laces, and looked back to her for directions. She had gotten the bandage securely around his head. She went to the girl and started to look her over. There was no blood, she just held her stomach and moaned.

I looked up at my name being called. "Petey, the ledger is gone. We have to fix that now!" P screamed at me.

I looked up. *Holy fuck.* The layered scaffolding system was made of steel. The horizontal pieces are called ledgers and the vertical pieces are called standards. If you remove one of the horizontal pieces, it can become horizontally unstable if one of the standard legs is pulled. Someone had removed one of these ledgers and the decks had dropped, and there was one in the air right above us.

I told one of the stagehands to grab a ledger on the deck and put it diagonally over the EMT and the victims for some protection.

I stood up, with the EMT action just off to my left and the guy who ran the production for the stadium on my right. Whenever there is a show in the stadium, this guy is the go-to for everything; he completely runs the HFS Festival from start to finish. He asked if I was alright and informed me that since this was an industrial accident, a state trooper needed to question me.

I looked at him and agreed, asking to just finish my cigarette before I went. I take the last drag of my cigarette, threw it away, and then lit another. I walked toward the twenty-yard line and saw a female state trooper. I got a chill; it was a cold DC night with the temperature in the sixties, but the humidity was up and I was slimy with sweat. I had goose bumps as I walked over to them. I was introduced to the trooper and I gave my name. The production manager touched me on my shoulder, gave a nod and walked off.

I dropped my cigarette and lit another. I took a really heavy drag, held it, and then exhaled. The trooper began to ask me questions about the accident: "Did you see it? What did you hear?" I took another long drag on my cigarette, tossed it away, and lit another. Then someone tossed me a T-shirt. That's when I noticed that I wasn't wearing mine; I used it on that guy's head. Here I was, giving an interview to this female trooper, shirtless, with fully erect nipples and goosebumps all over my chest. I think she was a little embarrassed for me.

I put on the T-shirt, and noticed blood on my hands, from his head. I took another long drag of my cigarette and tossed it away. The trooper asked me a few more questions, thanked me and suggested I go back to my hotel and try to sleep. I thanked her, nodded my head, and smiled; I told her I was going to try. It was 6:45 a.m. and I had not slept a wink. It was July 11 and the summer was just halfway over.

I spent the rest of July and the beginning of August with this team, doing gigs throughout the country, and then we rolled into Syracuse for my last gig of the season, the Great New York State Fair. I worked the whole fair and then took the stage down. I always enjoyed the fifteen-minute ride home from the fair.

I went back to doing local gigs. I had eliminated most people in my life except for Larry, Peter, and Nick, but only talked to them on the phone. I just didn't call back or reach out to anyone else. If I was not working, I was alone, drinking, in this studio apartment I was renting. I cared a lot about my friends and family, just not about myself. And I was beginning to not care about not caring, which is extremely dangerous. I kept to myself and my nights were spent thinking about whatever my brain chose, but it was never anything nice. My brain made me recount past events, as if to provoke me. Life in general was getting harder.

In October, my dad called me over to talk. He looked like he had just been kicked. "Your grandmother is moving out of the house and going to live with your uncle and cousins."

"Whoa, what?" I responded. "When was this decided?"

"I don't know, I just found out myself."

Apparently it had been decided that she would move to an assisted living facility in my uncle's city. They never talked to my dad about any of it, it was just dumped on him as the way it was going to be. He told me they were going to need my help moving things and cleaning the house after she left; I told him I would do whatever was needed.

Don't get me wrong, I was glad to see her go. I just couldn't believe we were left out of the loop.

A week later, I went over. My grandma was in the living room, on the phone with someone. When I looked around, I saw little round colored stickers on everything. I wandered around the house while she was chatting on the phone. Everything had a sticker on it. When she was done, I walked into the living room.

"I hear you are moving, old lady, what's up with that?" I asked with a smile.

"Well, yes," she replied with a hoarse little laugh. "While you're here, pick out something of mine you would like to keep."

"Okay." I asked about an item, she said it was taken. Then I asked about something else and that was taken. Finally, I asked about the egg.

She smiled and said, "I knew you were going to ask for that."

My grandmother owned a marble egg that sat on a small, three-legged gold stand. When I went to her house as a child, I would always tilt the egg up and try to get it to stay. I moved the things that she needed moved, grabbed my egg, and told her goodbye. (My father later relayed to me that he was given no choice of anything to keep from the house. He said his parents threw away all his childhood stuff when he went away to college.)

About a month later, my cousins came and moved my grandmother out. I never said goodbye. I went over after to clean the house for my dad and walked around a bit; it was empty, cold, and eerie without the furniture and Oriental rugs. I could not fucking believe she was up and gone. I went and sat on the stairs going up to the second floor, smelling mothballs from the attic.

My disbelief was welling inside. I was thinking about all the times we had dinner here. My grandmother never said she loved me, nor did I ever hear her say she loved anyone. I sat and cried. Our moving to this town, for her, had an adverse effect on me and my siblings. Now she was gone from the scene of the crime.

Pissed now, I went in to clean. I was down in the basement when my dad showed up and moved over to the fruit cellar. (My grandmother's house was built around 1919.) Inside were some old tools that belonged to my grandfather, a wrench and ball-peen hammer. There were a few mason jars, probably older than me. At some time I am sure they held the rhubarb jelly that my grandmother made, which I loved. I left those things for the new people.

My dad and I walked up to the living room and I gathered up the cleaning supplies. He was just walking around; I cannot imagine what he was thinking. The first eighteen years of his life were in this house and some of them were the hardest of his life. He came back to his mother because she was in her time of need, and twenty-seven years later she'd upped and left.

We locked the front door and put the key in the realtors' box and closed it. My dad closed the screen door behind him, then gave a sigh and got in his car. I followed him back to his apartment, dropped off the supplies, and saw my mom. My parents had had to move out of their house because my dad could not afford the mortgage anymore. He was underemployed and my mom had not worked in years. I was too drunk to care.

My mom's health had been deteriorating steadily. She had limited mobility and my dad has been taking care of her at home, while also working. I spent a few minutes with her, then left and went back to my studio. I got blind drunk for about three days. I was slowly hollowing out, boxing myself in, and trying not to associate with anyone if I could help it.

On Christmas Eve that year, Peter's parents had a party after his dad performed 10 p.m. mass. His father is an ordained minister and this event had been going on for years. Larry and I always went together and met Peter around 11:30 p.m. A lot of the kids that used to come had now graduated and were off on their own, so the party was smaller, yet still fun.

After the holidays, I just kind of drifted and kept to myself. I was waiting for the spring call to go back on the road and ignoring my own self-destruction.

I got the call in early April and did a couple shows for the George Strait show again. On his tour were Lee Ann Womack, Alan Jackson, Lonestar, Brad Paisley, and Sara Evans. We opened up in Raymond James Stadium in Tampa, Florida. It was a similar stage as the last tour, just a little smaller.

Around 3 p.m. on the first day of the build, I was just standing downstage, smoking a cigarette, when *BOOOOM!!* I immediately hit the deck and looked around. A bunch of other people had too and we were all looking around and trying to find the source of the noise. I looked up at the pirate ship (Tampa Bay's football team is the Buccaneers) located in one of the end zones and noticed it had wisps of smoke around it.

We got up, still looking around. I ran into a groundskeeper and asked what was going on. Apparently, the stadium gives tours to the public and sometimes they set off the cannon that they use for touchdowns, during tours. The show went on.

It was a short tour with a lot of driving. After Tampa, we drove all the way to Las Vegas for a show at the speedway, and after that was Little Rock, Arkansas. Then we finished up at Williams-Brice Stadium in South Carolina. I just kept withdrawing into myself more and more, drinking myself to sleep every night. After the tour, I went and did a few one-offs before heading to Washington, DC.

In DC, I worked the 2001 HFS Festival and this year for the first time it would be two days, back to back: Fatboy Slim, Green Day, the Cult, Fuel, Coldplay, Linkin Park, Lifehouse, Stabbing Westward, Good Charlotte, and many others. It was a great two-day event, the most bands they have ever had. I always watched all the shows of the events I participated in. I usually worked the day of the show, but if the weather was nice I had little to do.

After HFS I went to East Troy, Wisconsin, for the Ozzfest. The rest of the summer went on, one show after another. I was not even paying attention to where I was anymore. The summer ended back at the Great New York State Fair with Aaron Carter, Journey, Joe Cocker, Brad Paisley, Tim McGraw, Lee Ann Womack, and a few others. The gig ended, and I went back to my place.

I was a complete and utter mess. I was an alcoholic and I didn't care how I felt and what it was doing to me. To say I was of human form would be a major overstatement. At this point I was just a bag of bones just trying to get by in life. I avoided my parents and called Peter and Nick and they could hear me dying. Nick and Larry suggested I move to Boston, where they were. Larry had lived there for about four years already and Nick had moved there from New Orleans for graduate school for acting.

After the New Year, in 2002 I finally decided to move to Boston. Nick and his wife were going somewhere and would be driving through Syracuse and would pick me up. I could not look either of them in the face; I was so ashamed of myself. I hated myself. I must have emanated an aura of someone who was done with society and didn't care what happened to me.

We got to Boston and I stayed at Nick's for a couple days, then moved over to Larry's apartment. I was in horrible shape, but alcoholism presents a great shield of denial, for the drinker. I applied for some jobs, but I am not even sure how I would have made it through an interview. I had hit rock bottom and did not care. There was nothing I could give myself, so anything I gave anyone else would have been disingenuous. My hollowness was not some smooth piece of glass, or a cement swimming pool. I was cut, chipped, broken, and bleeding inside—jagged from everything I had done to myself. Every time my mind decided to take me on some spin, it took a piece of me and burnt it.

In the spring, Nick and his wife had me and Larry over for a barbeque at their house. They had an intervention for me, which only lasted about five minutes because I agreed to go to rehab. I wanted to stop feeling the way I was feeling, and felt guilty for these two having to deal with my sorry ass. A couple days later I went to a treatment program that Nick's aunt knew about.

Half of my life
I spent doing time for
Some other fucker's crime
Other half found me stumbling around
Drunk on burgundy wine[10]

If someone suggests that you need to go to rehab, go. It is one of the hardest things to do, because it immediately changes your world. But that's the whole point: your world isn't working, so you need to entirely flip your script.

It is one of the hardest things I have ever done. I went for two weeks; decided I was fine, which is not uncommon, and left. I was back in two weeks—because it turns out you cannot cure in two weeks what took twelve years to create. So, let us start with the second attempt.

The rehabilitation center was somewhat secluded, with a hospital right next door. You walk in the front door, fill out a form if you can, and they start to take your vitals. This center didn't discriminate and took all patients with addictions. Since I was abusing alcohol, I was put in a hospital bed and given the drug Librium, which is used to keep alcoholics from seizing up while they physically withdraw from alcohol. Alcohol is the only addiction where you can die from withdrawal. All other drug withdrawals just make you want to die.

I'd had a seizure when I was out on the road the summer before and went to the hospital. I blamed it on being dehydrated. I was swimming in denial and didn't care about the sharks.

After a day or so in bed, I was released into the complex: a single-floor building that had a big common room, a cafeteria, several conference rooms, and dorm rooms on either side of the complex, male one side, female the other. You have one roommate and you share a bathroom with the room next door.

The first two days, while lying in that bed, all I could do was think about was how many people I had disappointed: my parents, my brother and sister, Nick, Larry, Peter, BB, SW, and all the friends I had systematically cut out of my life. The list went on and on, from personal to professional. Mentally, the first few days of rehab were very hard for me. A million times, I stepped right into a mental noose and tried to drop. Self-mutilation and destruction at its finest.

It was a very dreamlike place for me in the beginning. I didn't want to talk to anyone. I was given a counselor who I would be having both private and group meetings with.

The day started off with breakfast and then a meeting. You can give money and a shopping list to the administration and they will go out and buy what you need. If you set foot off campus, you are gone for good.

Next, we would break off into groups and work for about an hour. Then we'd all take a break, maybe hang out in the back courtyard.

Whatever your assumptions about rehab are, you should just forget them. It is not whacked-out junkies who have lived in squalor—they would be very lucky to make it into rehab. Kids, moms, dads, grandmothers—anyone you can think of in society, they were in there. Middle-class white male heroin addicts, a stage 4 cancer survivor, a middle-aged librarian, a business man who sold a bunch of businesses for $9 million and was now sitting next to me, instead of enjoying his financial windfall. I met moms, hustlers, scared new dads. I saw a glimpse of society that I had seen every day, and they were dying just like me. And me, I was dying just like them. That is the common theme: not the drugs or booze, but the pain and fear.

If you could imagine my mind in a physical form when I walked into this facility, it would be: gunshot wound to the chest, severe head wound, pupil fixed and dilated, broken jaw, four crushed vertebrae, both legs broken, severe lacerations to the face, neck, arms, and legs, plus some dry skin. I was so mentally wrecked and the beginning of rehab just tosses you about like a ship on an angry ocean. My mind just raced. Guilt, shitloads of fucking guilt. It is so hard to shake in the beginning, and honestly, for some years after. The people who I disappointed were always on my mind, something I could not shake.

After a few days I got to know some people, just sitting around or out smoking a cigarette. Everyone has stories. You hear things in rehab that will shake you to your core: things people lost, got taken, or just faded away. People's pain, fear, and desperation. The one thing that every single person in that complex had in common, along with most of the counselors, was that none of them wanted to be an addict. Not one person at any time, in any of these facilities I would live in for the next twelve months, said that this was what they wanted for their lives, or the lives of their friends and families.

And another thing about addiction treatment facilities: people are always coming, or going. Static is never ever in the vocabulary. I was a loner for a few days, which was great, and then I got another roommate. He was a nice guy and after dinner I hung out and talked with him. He was a former medic from Vietnam and presently an EMT. He was in for benzodiazepines. When you leave rehab, you know a lot about other people's drug habits and their effects.

One night, I had a new roommate. I stayed up and played cards for a while, then went to sleep at curfew, 10 p.m. I crept in so I didn't wake him; the first night of rehab is tough and I didn't want to make it any harder on the guy. I got changed and crawled into bed.

Suddenly, I was awakened by a loud groaning: like a lawn mower trying to be started with wet grass in the shoot. I looked over and it was my roommate, in a full-blown seizure in his sleep.

I bounced out of bed and flew out the door and down the hall toward the nurse's station, yelling. Bolting down the hall, I put my hand up to push through the door—and *bam.* I had run full-steam into the door as it opened toward me. I hit the door so hard, I saw the nurse jump to her feet through the chicken-wire safety glass in the door. I opened the door and yelled, "A seizure, my roommate is having a seizure, hurry!"

I turned around and ran back to the room. He was still on his bed and his face was clenched, body gesticulating back and forth. Two hospital personnel came in with equipment and told me to leave. I went out into the hallway, stood there and waited, until the gurney was wheeled around the corner and into my room.

A couple minutes later he was wheeled out, his eyes wide open with a half-smile stuck on his face. I walked into the room as the medical team were leaving and an administrator was in there, securing his personal effects and clothing. He looked up and asked if I was alright. I nodded. He put my roommate's bag on his unmade bed. "He had a seizure, but we won't know until they look at him if he suffered any neurological damage. Try and get some rest." He shot me a soft smile, grabbed the bag, and walked out. I was sure he had given similar reports before.

I looked over and saw his unmade bed, and the sound he made ran through my head, and would continue to all day. After a few hours in bed, I got dressed and walked to breakfast, made my way over to the line. It was then I noticed that pretty much the whole room was looking at me, like seventh grade all over again. I grabbed some food and beelined it to an empty table, my eyes never leaving the ground. I didn't want to see that look again. I ate as quickly as I could, but I could hear people talking about me.

We went through the regular morning routine and my counselor and I discussed my roommate. Seizures are one of the side effects of benzodiazepines, he told me. All of the counselors there were addicts too, except maybe a couple of the clinicians and top administration. One counselor got arrested by his own drug task force, which he was the captain of.

I would never see my roommate again, though I heard he was okay. I was there for another week or so before I went to a transitional facility—a place before a halfway house, where you move after rehab, once you have some wits about you. This place was a house next to a cranberry bog. It was a bit more laidback; the new people were coming from other facilities, not straight off the streets.

The gentleman who was the day manager was a good guy and an amateur magician. He would put his cigarette out in his hand, do card tricks, and sleight of hand. It brought some good levity in a situation where it can be hard to find any happiness or joy. I was in a better place than I had been two months ago, but I still got overwhelmed by huge waves of guilt and fear.

The guy who worked during the nights was cool. As long as we were quiet we could play cards. It was here that I learned to play the eighteenth-century card game Whist, which is commonly played in United States prisons. The guys I played with had all been in prison. One said he ran on the perimeter of some of the Charlestown bank-robbing crews, was a complete cokehead, and this was his fifth or sixth rehab, he didn't remember. Then there was the first person I met who was court-mandated to a rehab program. He claimed he was there on drug and gun charges. If he completed his whole time in a program, the charges would be cleared. The third guy was just an ordinary addict, working a day job in construction. I was the odd man out, never arrested. But trust me when I say there was no difference between any of our addictions, and that is an important point.

I was in that facility a little over two weeks and then would transition to a halfway house for nine more months, on the coast of Massachusetts in September of 2002. Taking a "time out" in my life was the only way to fix my problem.

There were two houses on top of a hill in a residential neighborhood, with a shared driveway. The house on the right was more like a frat house than a regular house. You walked in and you were standing in our dining room/AA meeting room, which held six tables of about five people each. In the back corner were the public phone and the stairs going up to the bedrooms. One large bedroom held three people, a couple of singles, and then a couple of doubles. The bathroom was at the top of the stairs.

The other house was a large house that had been remodeled. It had administrative offices downstairs and three bedrooms upstairs, all doubles.

When I first arrived, I went through the entrance process: hand over all electronics, get list of house rules, and go over standard operating procedures. I hung out in the dining room until dinner. During dinner, guys came up and introduced themselves to me. I was put in the three-bedroom in the frat house. One other new guy was in there with me and a guy who had been there for a few weeks.

The next day I met my counselor, a real nice man from Massachusetts who had worked there for about five years. We went over what was expected from me as far as counseling was concerned. After a few weeks I would be expected to get a job. I had to go to a certain amount of AA meetings a week, and monthly we had a meeting at our house to attend.

There was a wide variety of guys there, most were from Massachusetts, but some from out of state like me. It was good to be away from home. Some guys were professionals whose addiction had finally caught up with them—construction, an architect, a restaurant manager. Some were guys who lived on the street, in flophouses and shitholes. A few of these guys were snowbirds, people who go into rehab so they don't have to be on the streets for winter. Once spring hits, they walk out of whatever facility they're in and go back to what they were doing. One guy told me he had been doing that for twelve years.

On the second day, I wrote my parents and siblings and told them where I was. It was the most humiliating letter I had ever written. Once again, I was going through the same mental shit I did the first few days of rehab: running through a list of everyone I had let down, friends, family, employers, everyone. The first few weeks were pretty rocky in the house—one person kicked out and another four left. This would be a common theme for the next nine months.

I was put over in the main house after a few weeks, into a double with a guy named Bill from Billerica. If you are from the Boston region, you know just how that sounded when he said it. He was a good guy, funny, but very weathered. He had some hard years on him and he was not much older than me, maybe ten years. He looked like someone tied him to a pier and let the sun and the waves have their way.

One of the guys who worked at the local Sears was leaving his job, and I went and applied. I got the job, working in their automotive department, in the tire section. It was an easy gig and the mechanics I worked with were nice; they loved my rock and roll stories. The mall was about two miles away, so I would walk to and from each day, weather permitting. It was the only exercise I got. I was still smoking cigarettes, which was not helping.

Time went on; more people left and more people came into the house. Trying to start a friendship was almost impossible. Guys came back from their weekend furloughs drunk; one guy was shoplifting from the store he was working at in the mall and trying to sell the goods to guys in the house. Other times, someone would just walk into their room, pack their things, and walk out. Unless you were court-ordered, you could leave whenever you wanted with no repercussions, except maybe to your health and sobriety.

Around the end of March, my roommate Bill came home and I could hear him downstairs as I lay in my bed before dinner. He was completely drunk; I could hear his loud talking and slurs. It took him about five minutes to get upstairs to me, and I grew sadder and sadder as each minute passed. I knew once he got to our room, he was going to have to pack and leave immediately, or the police would be called. That was the standard operating procedure of clients who were under the influence.

When he walked in the room, he leaned up against the doorjamb and then walked in and sat at the edge of his bed. I sat up on my bed.

"What's up, man? How are you feeling?"

Bill looked at me and his head wobbled. "I'm drunk, as you can see," he said matter-of-factly.

I just sat and looked at him for a minute; he had three weeks to go and he had just been talking about it last night. I looked at him. "You going to pack now?" I asked sheepishly.

"Yeah, I better," he said in his heavy Massachusetts accent.

I sat there and watched him drunkenly pack his things, not much other than clothes. Bill had been in the battle for about twenty years at this point. I really liked him. He and I and a few other guys would talk baseball, me being the only Yankee fan. He was a Carl Yastrzemski fan and so was my grandmother.

Bill gathered up his bag and put on his hat. I got up and gave him a hug. I asked him if he had a place to stay, but he just shrugged his shoulders.

He turned to walk toward the door.

"Hey," I said.

He turned and looked at me; I tossed him a half-pack of cigarettes.

"You sure?" he asked, all wobbly, which would have been funny if it was not so fucking sad.

"Yes, I have enough to kill me. Be well, Bill," I said and sat back down on the bed.

He thanked me, gave me a faint wave, and disappeared around the corner. I heard him trip and catch himself, letting out a "Shit" while going down the first few steps. I heard him saying goodbye and our counselor, M, walked him to the end of the driveway. I didn't watch, I just sat and thought about every single person I had disappointed on my way to this room.

Other people, I didn't mind if they left or got kicked out. I was trying to heal myself as best I could under those conditions, and they were a distraction. There were a few guys who I wanted to make it because I had heard their stories and wanted them to find some peace. This was just part of the ups and downs of living in a place like this. Here you are, trying to stand, and people around you are slipping and falling. You just hope that you don't get your legs kicked out from underneath you.

One Monday, it was late and we were in the dining room playing cards. A game was on TV and someone called over to me and asked if I wanted to watch. I looked up and saw Syracuse was in the NCAA men's basketball championship game. I said no and went back to playing cards. I didn't want to watch a game I should have been at, with my friends. I didn't want to be reminded of a city full of people I had let down. I read about the game the next day; Gerry McNamara and Josh Pace won the game by scoring above their averages.

There's a point in a facility like this when you want out. I had made the conscious decision to be there for the sake of my health, but after a while I wanted to escape. I had about a month and a half to go. I had reached out to the staging company I'd worked for and was going to go out on the road for the summer again.

Around this point, people begin to feel pressure about going into the real world again. A lot of the guys would bug out and leave or do something to get booted. You keep getting new cycles of people and they all go through "break-in" periods like I did, have to figure out whether they want to really be here. It is very hard to keep witnessing this cycle.

From the time I arrived until I left the halfway house, I counted fifty-four people, including myself, who came and went from the house. Only four of us "graduated" and the other fifty left or got kicked out. If you told me that every person I met in that facility had since succumbed to their disease, I wouldn't be shocked. I am an anomaly and I know it. I was staying and "graduating," no matter how rough it got.

When I made the conscious decision to get sober, it gave me a sense of relief. Addiction is a job, both in trying to hide, plus living in the nightmare itself. Alcohol, along with anxiety, made me withdraw from anyone that would stop me from drinking. Once I had a few months of sobriety, I knew I had made a good decision.

But being sober turned into a job for a while. It was 24/7 of not wanting to disappoint anyone. I did not want to drink again because I did not want people to think I was weak, or lazy. I did not want to show my face because of the shame I felt. It took me quite a while to realize it was not my fault. I did not intentionally want to become an addict. No one does. It is easy to become an addict when your own mind is conspiring against you.

CHAPTER 15

I went to Nick's house for a few days and then left for the Beale Street Music Festival in Memphis, Tennessee. This festival falls under a larger event called Memphis in May, down by the waterfront along the Arkansas River. It's a nice festival with multiple stages—a favorite of mine, due to the layout of the site and the mix of music. I got there Saturday and saw a few bands before heading back to the hotel to eat. I would be working the whole day and night on Sunday, so I wanted to try and sleep some.

Then I just jumped right back into the job. It was weird being back out in society, and the daily anxiety of falling down and having a drink was always on my mind. I worried constantly about failing—myself and the ones who supported me. It was a constant that stayed with me for a long time.

Sunday morning came a lot faster than I wanted it to. It was overcast, but not cold. Winds and sprinkles had been threatening something bigger. On Saturday I saw some of Willie Nelson's show and I saw Koko Taylor sing "Wang Dang Doodle," and I could not really ask for more in life. I missed Ratdog, Bob Weir's band outside of the Grateful Dead. The Sunday show had a great lineup scheduled, LL Cool J, ZZ Top, B 52's, Robert Randolph and the Family Band, Cross Canadian Ragweed, Jim Dickinson. Dickinson was a singer, record producer, and pianist who had done session work for several bands, including piano work on "Wild Horses" on the Rolling Stone album *Sticky Fingers.* His two sons, Cody and Luther, were also playing the show in their band, North Mississippi All-Stars. I got to see both, before the weather became sketchy.

LL Cool J and ZZ Top both ended up playing shortened sets.

I remember being in the trailer when ZZ's stage manager and the local production team were discussing their set and the duration of it. Conversations like these can get very contentious. One side is aware of contracts, others speak up for safety, and usually the band just wants to play. Super fun to watch!

I ended up in one of our staging trucks, getting a little rest before the overnight shift. When we—two climbers and two ground people—started out the following morning, we were not removing all of the stages. One of them and a bunch of other structures were staying for at least another week. We took out two of three baby stages and some other accessories, and were finally done at about 9 p.m. that night.

I spent the next few weeks traveling, and doing one-off shows, and then I headed to DC for the 2003 HFS Festival—which I didn't know then would be my last HFS Festival ever. It was the same build as usual, with Jane's Addiction, Godsmack, Chevelle, Jack Johnson, Switchfoot, and the Roots on the bill, along with a bunch of other bands.

Next I did the Celebration of Flight in Dayton, Ohio, on a plot of land downtown right next to the river, in a new park created for it. We had to build two full stages and three other small ones in about two weeks. Every day it seemed something else popped up to be done. They didn't provide us with climbers, because most times these city and state gigs are bare-bones events, so I felt like I spent half the time up in the air and the other half either on a forklift, when I could find one, or on a golf cart driving to another stage. Our site was twelve acres in size, not including the baseball stadium located a few blocks away, so walking was out of the question most of the time. There were some logistical issues too: not enough forklifts, and a steep incline.

The summer ended with me setting up the stage for the Delaware State Fair. Not my usual stomping grounds for this time of year, but I didn't live in Syracuse anymore. I actually didn't live anywhere as of that moment. I flew from the Philadelphia airport back to Boston, where Nick picked me up from the airport and we went out to dinner. He had finished grad school and was moving to New York City to follow his acting career. I told him I would tag along; I didn't really have a plan and my sister lived in the city. She would be excited to have me that close. I helped pack up Nick's house and helped move him and his wife to New York City.

I had been to New York several times in my life, but hadn't really thought much about living there. It definitely is not for everyone and it takes some adjustment. While I looked for an apartment, I lived with Nick and his wife for a while, during which the August 2003 blackout went down. Nick was out of town, and Peter was in town for a friend's wedding.

Peter was going to stay at Nick's for a night and then go to the wedding in Connecticut the next day. That day, Peter and I were going to meet a friend, taking a cab over to Madison Avenue where he worked. About three blocks away, suddenly we were stuck in the middle of an intersection, with the light out.

We paid the cabbie and got out to walk. People were streaming out of the buildings; all the power was out in the city and the buildings were emptying quickly. When our friend came out, he confirmed that the city was out of power and the cell phone lines were jammed. We decided to head to the west side to see if the PATH trains to New Jersey were running.

The three of us walked over to the Westside of New York, which was a blast. Pedestrians had completely taken over Eighth Avenue, heading to either ferries, which were going to take hours, or to walk out of the Lincoln Tunnel. Once we got to the Westside, we parted ways with our friend and headed up to West 72nd.

Peter and I walked up Tenth Avenue, with him wondering how he would get out of the city the next day. We assumed at that time that the blackout was just in the city. It took us about an hour to get home.

Nick's wife, JB, was in the apartment when we got there. It was a tough eight flights up the stairs and she shared our pain because she just gotten in with the dog. She had heard on the radio that it was not just New York City, but the entire northeast. We opened all the windows in the house, to try and cool it. We could get a breeze at that height, but it was still hot city air.

There was not really much to do. JB was a little worried for Nick. Peter did what he does best times of crisis: nap. JB and I hung out while Peter snored the last few hours of the afternoon away. When he woke up, he exclaimed he was hungry and that we should eat. We looked out the window and the streets were relatively empty of cars, but people were milling about.

We were moving into dusk and I volunteered to go find food. I walked down the eight flights and out into the New York City darkness, following the smell of smoke and grilling. Past Broadway, there was a large group of people in the street on West 72nd, with smoke from food cooking!

The grills were being manned by the local Hatzalah, a volunteer Jewish emergency medical service in New York City and other large cities in the US. The restaurants on the street were dumping their refrigerator and freezer contents onto the grills, creating a pay-as-you-go street barbeque. It was quite a sight— you don't come across such things in New York City on a regular basis. Some people just sat on the sidewalk and ate, while others grabbed food and went back to their homes. I would have loved to hang out on the street to eat, but I had my friends to think of, and grabbed my food to slowly walk back. I loved seeing the city in all its darkness. I will probably never see it that way again.

I made the long haul back up the stairs and popped into the apartment with the food. We sat at the table and went to work. Peter wondered aloud about how he would get to the wedding. The cell phone towers were still jammed with everyone trying to call in and out of the city. Not until a few hours later when JB and Nick talked, did we find out that the power outage was much bigger than we knew.

The next morning, Peter was able to get through to his friend and learn that the wedding was still on. He got a number and called a bridesmaid who had not yet left the city and she agreed to give him a ride to Connecticut. Crisis averted. JB and I went out to brunch, as some parts of the city had limited power and gas stoves. Nick was able to make it back to the city the next day.

I stayed with Nick and JB for about a month or so before I found an apartment up on West 116th. I moved in there and would eventually end up with two roommates, both women.

I got a job at Hostos Community College in the Bronx, at the International Alliance of Theatrical Stage Employees (IATSE). It was Local 1 I was working for, as they covered this part of the city. I was running spotlight for this Latin Jazz musical on at the college.

I worked in the theater for a couple of months, working the musical and other events. One night we had a jazz band from Cuba come play, but we had to wait for them to clear customs and were not sure the show would go on. Matt Dillon, the actor, was in the audience. He planted himself on the aisle, second row, so he could see the whole band. Finally these four "older than the mountains" Cuban men sauntered onstage, acknowledging the wild applause. They sat at their instruments and fiddled with their tunings. After a couple of minutes it grew silent and, with a simple nod, magic flew into the air.

These elder statesmen of Cuba put on such a show. It was tight, clear, and beautiful. I didn't know a song, nor had I have ever really listened to this music before, but it was raw, and powerful, with musical and cultural influences that date back hundreds of years. Music is and always will be an expression of history.

As we were shutting down the lighting booth, I noticed that Matt Dillon had made his way to the stage, with a group of people waiting to talk to the band members. Matt hung out while people said hello, waiting for the crowd to thin out. Finally, he approached the lead singer and put out his hand to shake it. The band had no idea who he was but were surprised and elated when he whipped out a couple of their albums.

Matt stood and talked with the members of the band, each

coming by and introducing themselves, looking at the albums and throwing their signatures on them. After a few minutes Matt said his goodbyes, beaming happily.

Then Bill Clinton came to the college for the William Clinton Presidential Foundation Young Adult Symposium on increasing young adult activism. There were speakers during the day in both the main and small theaters, plus the added security for the ex-president. I had gone through the security check before, while working for the other staging company in Pennsylvania. They take your license and run it through a database and if the government dings you back, you cannot be onsite to work.

It was a pretty crazy day, dealing with so many moving parts of security and outside production, plus the people from the Clinton Foundation. What makes a situation like this hard is the movement of the ex-president. All ex-presidents have a Secret Service security detail that follows them everywhere they go. When an ex-president comes to a public event, their security blossoms into what is basically a thirty-foot no-go zone.

Then there were also Bronx police and S.W.A.T, local Homeland Security detailed to New York City, and whatever other government agency was assigned to keeping New York City safe. When the ex-president walks, this zone of ringed security moves with him and makes sure no one breaks the zone.

There was a spill offstage in the small theater and I went to grab a mop between the backstage of the small theater and main room and woodshop of the main theater. I got that quickly cleaned up before someone with dress shoes took a digger. It is bad form having an ex-president take a fall on your wet stage.

I took the mop through the crowded offstage and wheeled it back. By the time I turned around and took two steps, there was a Bronx police sergeant standing right in the doorway. I took one more step and he palmed my chest, looking at me. "Sorry. You cannot go any further," he said while putting his arm down.

"No!" I said in a low voice. "Really?"

"Really. This is the back end of the security and the president just went onstage."

"I just need to squeeze around the corner and into the main room. I am not even going on stage."

But he was not having it. So, I was stuck in a mop closet for the next forty minutes or so while President Clinton spoke.

After the speech, he left the stage and moved into the theater complex. The sergeant looked at me and gave me the go-ahead. To this day whenever I smell old mop water, I think of President Bill Clinton. I had to recount my story to each of my fellow stagehands, all of whom loved hearing about my isolation and location. The next time we had an event in the theater, I was tasked with mopping the stage at the end. Very funny, mother-fuckers, very funny.

After a few other events, there was no need for my services at the theater anymore. I didn't have a union card and I wasn't sure I wanted to pursue one. I decided I wanted to find something more permanent, so I ended up getting a job with a small staging company with an office in Brooklyn, but based in London, building platforms in and around New York City. I had a solid 9-6 job, plus other gigs around town. I worked with some very nice people, which always makes a tough job easier.

Soon, I moved from the West 116th to East 83rd near East End Park. It was a good location, near the subway, the park near the river, and the restaurants on Second Avenue. I still worked at the staging company in Brooklyn, but I was beginning to get an itch for a college degree. Everyone in my family had one and I was embarrassed I didn't, feeling left out.

I kept working at the staging company while investigating going back to school. Living in New York City gives you a wide choice of schools to pick from. I had not been in a formal education setting since trying to take community college classes back in Syracuse, with miserable results. At that time, I was not built to be in school. I knew I would need to start back at a community college, because this was going to be a big switch in gears.

That August, I told the staging company I would no longer be working for them, as I was going back to school in the fall. They were cool about it and we decided I would work a few gigs in September and October, to lend a last hand and pick up a few bucks.

In September, I started back to school at Borough of Manhattan Community College, all the way down near the financial district in lower Manhattan. It was an easy train ride and a walk of a few blocks across town to get there.

I really loved going back to school. Around this time, not drinking allowed me to better focus on things in my life. I had not written anything formal since my freshman year in college, so my first papers were train wrecks. Another layer was wrapped around me when I started school, plus I noticed that my anxiety was rising at times. I was putting an extreme amount of pressure on myself to do well in school.

The second year, I had to get an internship for a business class, and also a job. I got a job at a financial services company in the chapter 11 bankruptcy field, doing administrative work: my first corporate 9-5 job in my life. It was definitely a big switch from my days of building stages and working events and I put a lot of pressure on myself to succeed here as well. I stayed with the internship and it turned into a full-time job as I finished up my last classes at the community college.

I also met my now-wife, online (because when you leave rehab, a bar is no longer a good place to hang out). Now, I know I haven't mentioned my sex life at all—because the people it involves deserve some privacy. Unfortunately, 95 percent of my relationships had ended up the same way: me breaking up with them. The back of my brain acted like an assassin, and when things got tight, someone had to go.

In most relationships, we look for the goodness in people, things that make us feel happy and safe. Part of my brain does not believe in such things. So as the relationship moved along and a woman became more empathetic and sympathetic, part of my brain determined that it was dangerous and I broke up with her, whether I really I wanted to or not. It was a very disturbing pattern but one I didn't recognize for years.

I'm not sure what was different about my wife; she was no more or less empathetic than most of the women I dated. Maybe my brain was just tired from running, and didn't have any fight left in it.

When she and I first met, we would IM each other during work. You can really get to know someone doing this. When we first started talking it was just basic stuff, but we eventually opened up a bit.

And then one day she asked me if I had anything else I wanted to tell her about myself, and I took a big fucking gulp. I was sick of how all my relationships had turned out: with me moving on, not really giving a good reason as to why.

So, I just blurted out in type that I was sexually abused as a kid. *Send!*

Holy fuck, what did I just do?

I could not believe I had just let the biggest secret of my life out. But I was sick of hurting women. I felt horrible for the way I had treated women in relationships.

After the IM was sent, I just sat there and waited. The little pen-like thing that shows she's typing moved about five times—but no message popped up.

Finally, she responded that she was sorry it had happened and if I ever wanted to talk to her about it she would give me an unconditional ear. I was expecting her to not want to be a part of it, but that was not what happened.

Still, I knew I had just pulled the pin out of a grenade—and I was the grenade. My wife is everything you want in a significant other: caring, kind, and sympathetic. To this day, I don't really know why my brain didn't turn her away.

CHAPTER 16

After a while of dating, at around age 35, I moved in with her and started thinking about where to get my bachelor's degree. I finally decided to go to St. John's University in Queens. It was the easiest in terms of school, work, and life. So my wife and I moved out to Queens. This was my first time living with someone—something to get used to. I was not good at it, and I'm still not.

It was an easy transition to the new school, just a bigger campus and buildings. One major drawback to Borough of Manhattan Community College was that many of the classrooms have no windows. It was nice to have a campus to walk around with different buildings, even though I really only went in three of them. I was a Sports Management major, so I also spent time in the athletic building. I was obviously older than my peers, but I didn't care. I got along great with my professors when I needed to engage with them. I must have been a breath of fresh air, since I was never going to them to complain or ask for an extension.

I was living with my future wife in Queens, going to school full-time, and working in the city at the financial services firm full-time. I managed the schedule as best I could, and we saw each other at the end of the day. On the surface, everything was fantastic. I was doing well in school for the first time in my life. I had a great roommate whose feet didn't smell and she liked me. I had a job, not what I wanted to do in life, but I was getting paid and worked with nice people. But inside, I was slipping through the cracks and drowning.

I would wake up almost every night at around 12:30 or 1 a.m., my mind running like a freight train. I hadn't had such serious sleep disturbances since I was a child. Now, I was getting between fifteen to twenty hours of sleep a week. I would wake up in fourth gear, waiting for the sun to come up so I could make coffee, about a pot a day before noon. I was afraid if I drank coffee after lunch it would affect my falling asleep at night.

My work at the financial services firm had me do research online and then disseminate that information to a team. Some days I would go into work and do this, then work the rest of the day. Other times I would do research early morning, go to school, and then go to work afterward. My early-morning work started to turn into 2 a.m. work. I needed access to the Pacer Service System, which holds all federal cases presently being adjudicated through the United States, which I could do it at any time with my code.

After sending out my 3 or 4 a.m. email to the group, I would either do schoolwork, or just watch TV. This went on through my last year of school, and until I told my wife recently, she had no idea I was living this way. I would either go to work in the morning, come home and go for a run, or go to the gym. If I had school that day, I would go to gym at school and then to my classes.

On Saturdays I would be up, make a pot of coffee around 6 a.m., have a cup, go to the gym, come home, and finish any schoolwork I needed to do. All of that was accomplished before 11 a.m., every Saturday. This went on for some time. My wife was oblivious to my struggles, because I was hiding it all, pretending everything was normal.

But I forgot that when you send an email, there is a time stamp, and I was sending emails to my team way before one should normally be working. One day my boss came up to me out of the blue and asked how I was doing. As usual, I responded with the time-tested "Great! Yourself?" but he was not having any of it. He gave me a side-eye, and I probably looked like I had escaped from the set of *Trainspotting*, but he let it go.

Having worked at the financial services firm for a few years, I started looking for a more defined marketing role. I applied for a marketing position at a law firm and got hired. It was an alright place. People seemed nice. I was given the financial services, banking, investment part of the marketing tasks—and then, on September 16, 2008, I was out of a job. The market blew up with the downfall of Lehman and my job just blew away with the wind. At this time, I was getting my MBA online through the University of Wisconsin public system, so I at least had something to do to keep me busy.

My wife didn't notice, but my anxiety began to ramp up even more. We got into fights and I knew it was because I was burnt-out. We had also begun planning our wedding, so that was another thing to think about at 1 a.m.

I remember when I applied for an internship at College Sports Network, owned by CBS. I went to their office on the Westside of New York. You walk in and you're in this small basketball court, which serves as a group meeting room, kind of cool. I then was brought in to meet the boss, and we started with what I was doing in school. Then she asked me how I would grow their station. I suggested appealing to parents of high school children.

She pushed a few things out of the way on her desk and put my résumé to the side. She then took out a piece of paper and started to write. "Slow down, what did you say?"

She then said she wanted me to meet the other head honcho there, so she brought me next door and introduced me to some Muppet who didn't even rise to shake my hand, or introduce himself; he basically didn't take his eyes off his computer screen. I sat down without him offering. He then asked me about the classes I was taking. I told him, even though he was not paying any attention to me.

After a few more minutes he called the woman back and we went back to her office. I was steaming pissed by this time, and wanted to walk out. I felt so fucking disrespected by these people and I didn't even work for them yet. We talked for another five minutes and then the interview was over.

As I was leaving she said to me "You should make nice with my secretary, she's the one who decides who gets the internships." *What?* This was such an embarrassment. It shook my confidence and made me seriously rethink everything I was doing in my life. I had wanted to see what the business world had to offer. Nothing, I guess, at least not for me.

My wife and I moved back to New Jersey, to be closer to her family. We lived in an apartment building across the street from James J. Braddock Park. I ended up getting another financial services job and hated everything about it. If not for the financial collapse I would never have worked there in a million years. It definitely added another layer. It sucks to work in a place you hate.

I was working full-time, going to school part-time, and still not sleeping. No matter what I tried, or what I changed, I just could not get a regular night's sleep. I had not slept for eight hours since long before I could remember, without the aid of booze, exhausting physical exercise, or work. No matter what I did, I was up, or I could not even go down, too wound up from whatever adventure my brain took me on. My brain would spin for hours, about something I did, or didn't do, or forgot, or almost forgot.

We ended up getting married without a hitch in a beautiful ceremony with no arrests. I hated my job, but I loved being with my wife. Her being a vegetarian improved my diet; I still ate meat, just not as much, which helped me to feel better overall. I was exercising, but it wasn't helping my sleep like it used to when I was younger.

My wife and I got into the conversation you get into after you get married—you know the one, about the little people. I knew my wife wanted kids, she had said so in passing. Up until the conversation, I didn't really have an opinion about children one way or the other—but I doubted my ability to be a good father. My childhood didn't really prepare me to take care of another human. I didn't want to have kids who grew up and got assaulted like me. I could not stand myself, so I didn't want to bring a child into this world, to be in the same position as me. But I saw how much this meant to my wife, and that was probably the biggest factor in me saying yes.

The anticipation of waiting for a birth is pretty weird. You have no idea what you might get. I was anxious about the baby's health, my wife's health, and whether I could even do the job. My skepticism added a new layer, one I never felt before. I questioned, daily, my ability to properly raise my son.

My wife was way off her normal game. She only wanted three things: her back to stop hurting, the baby out, and the pain in general to stop. It is very hard to be in that room when you're the person that put her in that state, even though you both enjoyed it nine months before. They love you and want to kill you all in the same contraction.

But I got to witness the birth of my son and cut his cord. I was a new dad! It was a really nice feeling to hold my son for the first time, a feeling I can never replicate again. Nothing feels quite like the first time with your first, just-out-of-the-oven child—talk about a new-car smell! I was in complete awe that I could make something so beautiful.

The hospital let me stay the night with my wife and child in her hospital room. It was tough, with just a small wooden bench to sleep on. My son let out a scream in the middle of the night and I let out a "Oh my god, this is a bad idea," not exactly reassuring my wife. I was angrier at that fucking bench than my son's scream. I felt it would have been better if I hadn't stayed.

I went home the next day to check on our dog and get things ready for my son to come home. I was excited about the whole prospect of being a dad. The first couple of days were hard, but harder for my wife. It was physically and mentally exhausting for her, and I tried to help out the best I could. I was spinning all over the place, trying to make sure things were done around the house and my wife and baby were okay.

A few days after we got home I went back to work. It is rather hard to sit at work and concentrate when your wife is at home with a newborn baby—especially when it's a job that you hate. Our families would come and visit over the next couple of weeks.

After a few months we started to look for a house, because our one-bedroom apartment was becoming too much of a hassle. In the meantime, my wife commuted to New York City every day with my son, and handed him over to her cousin, who took care of him while we worked. Then my wife and son would commute home. Apparently, he had a following of admirers by the time she stopped commuting with him.

My wife, son, and I moved to a small house south of New York City that we rented, with two bedrooms and a small attic. It was convenient for commuting and traveling to visit friends and relatives. My wife's mom became the de facto child care provider for a while and it was my turn to commute with my son. I would drive him to my work, and my mother in-law would meet me in the parking lot to pick up and drop off my son. My mother in-law loved taking care of my son and it allowed him to bond with his grandmother.

When my son was a little older, we found a local woman with a home daycare. It was very convenient because her house was en route to the train station, so my wife could drop him off and pick him up with ease. And Kathy was great with my son. He learned to count to twelve by age two, by crawling up the stairs of her house and counting the steps.

With my son, another layer was added to my life. I was now responsible for my life, the life of my child, and the well-being of my wife. I wanted to do anything and everything to keep them happy and healthy, even if it affected my health, which I was used to not caring about. *Whatever happens to me, however I feel, so be it, as long as they're fine.* I wanted my son to grow up and not have to struggle like I had to, not go through the

pain, fear, and all the other shit that went along with my circumstances. He deserved better.

As much fun and pleasure as I had being a father, my anxiety level was rising because I had no idea if what I was doing
was right or wrong, plus I was keeping a hypervigilant watch out
for people who would want to harm my son.

When my son was two we had a birthday party for him.
I was wound up so tight, had not slept well, even by my standards, for weeks now. We were having the party at the local YMCA,
where I went to the gym and my son took swimming lessons.
On our way there, my wife asked me a question about something
and I just lost it. I came back at her like a ferocious dickhead.
Needless to say, my wife was beginning to suspect that something was wrong with me.

I knew something was wrong, but I didn't know what. I
was letting little things get to me and big things run over me.
I worked with people who were dirtbags and hated going there
every day; it was chipping away at me from the inside. Being
sober made it easier to see these things. Not trying to get my fix
meant I was better able to concentrate on what was important.

Around this time, my wife started to talk about having a second
child. This was a very tough conversation for me, even though I
didn't share that with my wife. Inside I was being torn apart. I
struggled with the financial burden of a second child, and something else, which cannot be bought: time. When you have a second child, the time you can spend with each child changes.

It took a while for my wife to convince me. I had a hard
time wrapping my head around the financial piece, because I
didn't want to be living on a shoestring budget like I had growing up. I wanted my children to have every opportunity I never
had.

But my wife's argument always included the statistics
of only children and the difficulties they experience in life.
After some serious soul searching, and a little pot smoking—I'd

started smoking pot a few years back to help with my anxiety—I agreed to try for another child.

When we decided to go forth and multiply, we also decided that we again needed a bigger place to live. So, while my wife was pregnant with our second child, we looked for a home for our expanding family, and found a place one town over from where I worked at the time. It was on a major bus line into New York City, so she'd have an easier commute to her nonprofit job. We both liked the house and its location and we decided to make the move.

My job was becoming more and more unpleasant. I had never worked at a job that I detested this much, and the people I worked with did nothing to soften the blow. Then, three months before my daughter was born, which they knew about, they let me go, citing a change in company direction. And they did it *two weeks before* my 401k vested, costing me about $250,000 in retirement, up in smoke. Thanks for nothing, assholes!

So, with my second child on the way and the US still in a bad economy, my wife and I decided I would take care of my daughter for a while, to help keep expenses down. This would provide me a chance to bond with her that I hadn't had with my son. There was a small victory to be had here.

Toward the end of October, we celebrated my son's third birthday. He had been great while my wife was pregnant. He was excited to have a baby sister and like most brothers, he hated her the minute she got home. The next couple of weeks were the same as my son's post-birth, but with less stress. The second child is always easier to deal with because you know the pitfalls and challenges.

Around the first week of December, my wife and I were woken up by our son screaming. I jumped out of bed and ran up to his room. I burst through the door and my son was upright in bed and throwing up. I ran over to him and held him as his little body convulsed from vomiting. My wife was right behind me. Holding him, I tried to calm him down and reassure him that he was going to be fine.

I got him out of bed and brought him to the bathroom, washed him up, and got him into new pajamas. I got new sheets and a blanket for his bed, stripped myself and put new clothes on. We got him to bed and I stayed for a little while to make sure he was okay. My wife went back to sleep in my daughter's room.

The next day, the boy stayed in bed and recovered. My wife and I were in the kitchen talking when suddenly, I grabbed the island with one hand and the rim of the sink with the other. I swung over to the sink, pushed a handful of dishes out of my way, and proceeded to vomit about two pounds of my life away.

I crawled to bed, while my wife was deciding what to do. I got a prescription of Zofran to help settle my stomach but I was very worried about my wife and daughter. If in five minutes this had brought me to my knees, what could it do to my daughter? I lay in bed for most of the day and at one time, my son crawled into bed with me and tried to help me feel better. My son bringing truth and justice to the streets of a Noro-virus.

I tried my best to get fluids and food into myself. I knew I had to do whatever it took to keep things going and make sure my wife and daughter didn't get sick. I spent that day dying and most of the next.

Then my wife started to show symptoms. She was tired from taking care of my daughter and didn't have the rest and food she really needed for the fight. That night, my wife told me she was deteriorating, that my daughter had thrown up and needed to go to the hospital. There was a snow storm bearing down on us and my wife was worried my daughter would dehydrate. I helped get her and my daughter ready the best I could.

Once the bag was packed, I realized I was about to send my wife and three-week-old daughter to a hospital. I was worried that I would never see them again.

My wife took them to the hospital where my children were born. She said it took about four times to get the IV into my daughter's arm; each time making my wife cringe. They finally got a line into my daughter and my wife finally relaxed, then she started throwing up all over the place and they fixed an IV in her.

I stayed home with my son and took care of him. He, of course, was better than any of us because he'd started it. After a couple of days my wife and daughter came home, and I will be forever grateful they made it home.

The next couple of months consisted of me and my daughter figuring out life. It was a good time, considering the circumstances. I would have preferred not to have my 401k stolen from me, but that's life. My daughter was a funny little baby. She didn't like her feet being covered, which almost got me into a brawl in a supermarket one day. I took her out to pick up a few items, sat her in a shopping cart. I left her feet exposed, even though it was winter, because she would become very upset if you covered them, a lesson I'd learned many times over.

I walked into the market and was looking at some things on a shelf when a man came behind me, grabbed my daughter's blanket, and put it on her feet.

I spun around. "What the fuck are you doing? Do not touch my daughter. Who the fuck do you think you are?"

He sputtered back at me. "I was just putting her blanket—"

"I don't give a fuck what you think you were doing. If you go near my daughter one more fucking time I will break your fucking face open. Got it, asshole?!?!"

He just stared at me. When I looked up I noticed the people behind the meat counter were staring at me and so were some customers. I didn't give a fuck. The man just looked at me and slunk away. As he was walking away my daughter kicked the blanket off her feet. That child wanted naked feet, so she was getting naked feet. Other than that, she was a pretty easy baby.

Our first few months together were fun, but tough. Since children don't really give you any solid responses until six months old, it can be hard to parent when you get no information other than crying.

I was also trying to get my résumé out there. During this time period, my use of marijuana increased. My wife was not too happy about that in the beginning. She was still in the mindset of marijuana as a gateway drug to cocaine, heroin use, and devil worshipping. But it was one of the only things, outside of exercise, that helped me deal with my daily stress.

Pot is not a gateway to anything but potato chips and late-night Woodman's games on ESPN. Alcohol, though—alcohol is the gateway drug. Not once have I been in a room with a bunch of people smoking pot, saying we should buy some cocaine. I have, however, been in a room with a bunch of drunks asking if we should go buy an eight-ball of cocaine. This is the reality and truth.

In January 2015, my wife and I decided to buy a consignment store and go into business. It had just come on the market and we thought it might be a good venture, since finding a job in the recession had been nearly impossible. My wife still worked in the city and I ran the store during the week; she worked at the store on weekends and I would take care of the kids. We hardly saw each other, and when we did we were exhausted.

The store eventually got too hard to operate. Fighting Internet sales proved too difficult. I enjoyed the experience and learned a lot, but it also took a heavy psychological toll on me. I was sleeping even more erratically than usual and feeling very stressed. We were living on one income, and I wanted and needed to work. I just wanted to find a job that I liked.

I did a little research and found a little staging/event company right near where I lived that was right up my alley and needed help. They used the same layered scaffolding that I had experience with, as well as hydraulic stages. I primarily worked around the tri-state area, so I wasn't away from my family for too long.

So, I'd finally gotten a job in a field I liked, doing what I like to do and making money, and my mental health was on the brink of breakdown. I was becoming a monster to my family, both verbally and physically intimidating. I would get nose-to-nose with my wife during arguments, or just follow her around the house demanding she talk or answer me. This was the last place I ever thought I would be.

And then I almost hit my son. My wife said something needed to change.

I could not tell her what was wrong with me, because there was nothing wrong. Of course, there was—there was something very wrong with me. My wife knew and she wanted to fix it. She suggested we go see a counselor together.

Nothing else was working for me. No conversation we had made me feel better, though she wanted and tried to help. And I had no choice if I wanted this marriage to remain intact. I was afraid if I didn't go, my wife might have taken drastic measures to ensure her safety and the kids'. See, I was still holding that grenade—if my wife filed for divorce I would have been screwed. I could lose access to my children. I didn't think my wife would use my mental state against me; I worried her attorney would, though.

So, I didn't have a choice but to go to the counselor. I wanted to get better, plus I was holding a fucking grenade in my lap—and I was the one who had pulled the pin. I think I'm addicted to the smell of sparks.

We found a therapist right near where we lived. He was a really nice guy, and good. We went to him a few times together and he provided us with some great tips for communicating. As he learned a little bit more about me, he suggested I go for some more treatment. He suggested I look for a therapist who used what's known as EMDR.

CHAPTER 17

I spent the next two weeks researching therapists who provided EMDR (Eye Movement Desensitization and Reprocessing). I performed some cursory research on this therapy, which is expressly meant to integrate trauma. It's a psychotherapy treatment developed by a woman named Francine Shapiro. While walking through a park one day, she noticed that her eyes darted back and forth when she thought of a past trauma she had suffered. As she began to research this action, she noticed that her anxiety subsided when the eye movements were brought under control.

I knew if I did too much research my brain would go on the defensive and I would try to self-sabotage, which I had been doing for years—so I stopped there. It was better to get an idea of what I was dealing with and then let the professional take over.

It was Tuesday, November 22, 2016, and my dad would be coming for Thanksgiving the next day, with my sister and brother in-law to follow the day after. It was a cold and wet night, miserable. This might sound weird, but central New Yorkers would rather it snow than rain. We can do things in the snow, but you don't want to do shit when it is wet and cold out.

I parked my car in the small parking lot of the nondescript building that held offices for several professionals: therapist, financial adviser, dietitian, and a few others that rented space. The parking lot was sparse, as it was going on 7:20 p.m. I had a 7:30 p.m. appointment and I hate being late. I went to the front of the building, climbed the few steps to the brown door, and opened it, greeted with a rush of warm air and protection from the rain.

I climbed the set of stairs in front of me and walked down

the hallway, checking the name plates on all the closed doors. As I came to the end of the hall, the last door on the right was open and the name of the woman I'd talked to on the phone was emblazoned on the door.

I walked into the room and was greeted with the hiss of a white noise machine. I was full of anxiety, wondering how I'd gotten there. *Because your life is falling apart and you've been verbally and physically intimidating your wife and kids.* Oh yeah!

I heard the crack of the door and two voices, their words drowned out by the white noise machine. A woman walked toward the door, zipping up her coat as she went.

The other woman looked at me with a warm, disarming smile and asked, "Hi, are you Peter? I'm Ann."

I stood up to shake her outstretched hand. "Hi," I replied and she invited me in.

The room had low light, with two large windows. Each corner of the room had a chair, with the door occupying the fourth corner. The chair in front of me was simple, with no arms and covered with fabric. The chair kitty-corner to me was a recliner, and the other was a wooden rocker with cushions on the seat and back. I stepped into the middle of the room and waited for further instruction.

I sat in the recliner and started talking to Ann about why I was there. EMDR involves a lot of breathing and I told her I had done yoga and could breathe through my diaphragm. I have used yoga in my exercise regimen for over a decade. I felt as though I was mentally wincing when I told her about Bruce. The anxiety in my body was pronounced.

The first session we spent just trying to find the anxiety in my body. My left eye would twitch when my anxiety rose; my chest would get heavy and my hand or fingers would twitch. My heart rate would jump and my hearing and eyesight would become more acute. I felt pressure in my shoulders and chest. Many of these symptoms were also exacerbated by my lack of exercise and sleep, which had been piling up over the last few years.

After my first session I felt horrible. I had never talked to anyone for that long about what happened—not my wife, friends, or family. I used my breathing the whole time, though, and it reminded me why I like yoga so much. My head was a mess, though, and my body felt like shit.

But I had finally done something about what happened to me, and now it was going to be dealt with, on my terms. My life had been dictated by something else since third grade.

It took a few sessions before I started to notice any changes. One thing was for sure—my subconscious didn't like someone poking around under the hood. It provided every obstacle it could to make that inquiry stop: self-doubt, doubt of Ann, doubt about whether I had the courage and fortitude to see this through. It was scary to learn that a part of my brain had, was, and would try to actively work against my health and well-being.

I was called into work a couple days after the New Year started, to load up all of our staging equipment because a group was heading down to Washington, DC, to prepare for the 2017 presidential inauguration. I remember sitting on my forklift, with a blanket across me, even though I was still wearing winter clothing. The site is located a few blocks from the ocean and it was breezy; you don't get much physical action just driving a forklift.

My phone rang and my dad's number appeared on the screen. The first thing that popped into my mind was Garrett's mom—the last time my dad had called me during the day. I knew something was wrong.

I answered my phone and my dad sounded subdued. He had just gotten off the phone with my sister and he told me that my mom was dead. Her body finally had just given up. She had been in assisted living for about ten years after the recurrence of breast cancer and her second mastectomy. He told me he didn't know when the funeral would be because she had donated her organs to science and then would be cremated.

I was sad my mom had passed, but it was expected. My mom was a good person and cared very much, but like my dad did not really take the time to get to know me. She had tried the best she could as a parent, but I'm not sure how equipped she was to handle it. After Bruce died, she just sort of coasted and it was exacerbated by Garrett's mom's death. I believe my mom (and dad) had a bunch of guilt about not being able to save my brother, but they never really thought about all the destruction he brought to me and my siblings. Once the mid '90s hit my mom just kind of gave up.

I told my dad I was sorry. He had been to the facility to see my mom almost every day, except when he came for Thanksgiving. My mom had suffered a bunch of mini-strokes, which had an adverse effect on her brain. Her moods would swing wildly, from just hanging out to full-on cursing at my dad, calling him a fucking asshole and saying it was his fault she was in the facility. She didn't remember that it was her choice to smoke, not exercise, and eat poorly. He would stay away for a couple of days and then visit again. He never knew what he would get.

It was hard visiting my mom in the facility. My family and I could only visit in short windows, due to my children possibly bringing in germs, or bringing them out. My dad wouldn't tell my mom when we were visiting, just in case we had to cancel. He did want to set up expectations and have them crushed. She was already in a fragile mental state.

In late March we headed to Syracuse for the funeral. I had told Garrett and Dan about her death right after it happened and let them know when the service would be. My mom liked both of them very much and always wished I was more like them.

The service was held at my dad's church, but with no calling hours beforehand, usual M.O. for Catholic burials. Dan and Garrett were there, along with Garrett's dad and wife, plus Dan's parents. Chris, Bob, and Jamie came, along with LG from the florist shop and another classmate, TE, which was an unexpected surprise. I was very happy to have their support.

After the service we went to the cemetery where my dad's

parents, my brother, and a couple of my dad's aunts and uncles are buried. We went inside the mausoleum to intern my mom. Inside was a wall of little metal doors, about eight by twelve inches in size. One of the doors was open and there were a few chairs set out in front of the space.

We waited for the priest to show and my dad placed my mother's remains in the wall. After a few kind words by the priest, the ceremony was over. Everyone went outside and was talking about next steps for the day. I took a quarter out, placed it next to the urn and closed the door. It would be the last thing I would give her. I took my knife out of my pocket, closed the door, and used the blade to screw and seal the door shut. And that was the end of my mother's life with me.

I didn't shed any tears that day. My mom had been in assisted living for so long, I always knew the inevitable was coming. Father Time is undefeated, no matter what steps we take to push him away. I had come to terms with my mom dying.

My mother was always a little aloof to me. The phrase "children should be seen and not heard"—I heard her say it when I was little and came to terms with the fact that she wasn't really interested in my life. She never took any actions to make me think otherwise.

That saying is one of the most dangerous I have ever heard. Now that I'm older I realize how it distanced me from my parents and how they really knew nothing about me. I know a lot about them, but they knew nothing of my loves, my fears, my ambitions, things that make me tick.

But you can only play the hand you are dealt. Luckily, I had gotten myself a new dealer.

A couple of weeks after I came back from the funeral, my therapist Ann gave me her diagnosis: anxiety and post-traumatic stress disorder (PTSD). She said I also probably rub up against a few other diagnoses, but don't meet the minimum requirements to be labeled. She said she could help me with my problems and I agreed.

A name. Finally, I had a name. I always knew things were wrong, but my logic was, once Bruce was gone, he could not hurt me anymore, and it only happened once for a short time, so it was no big deal. I was wrong, though, and now I had anxiety and PTSD.

After many discussions with Ann, I'm not sure if I suffered more harm from the abuse, or all the years of trying to keep it a secret. Not to mention my unstable and unsafe home environment, after it happened. Though I guess it does not really matter. This was where I was, and the bad feelings were coming out either way.

After each session, I felt mentally and physically exhausted. I had never done anything like this before and my mind was doing everything it could to prevent it from happening, to prevent me from engaging. My mind was telling me it was unsafe to do this. I was reliving a lot of mental pain, anger, and fear that had been packed away into my subconscious. I would go home and both kids would be in bed, which was good. I didn't want them to see me after these sessions because I was visibly shaken.

My wife quickly picked up on my cues and treaded gently around me. I tried to hide what was happening, but it's hard when you live together. Once again, I was trying to hide something, to avoid tough conversations with people, or them getting involved and worried. Old habits are hard to break, especially when they are in cahoots with a mental illness. I was now breaking a rule that I had created—and was discussing my abuse with a stranger, no less.

It was hard to transform this part of my life. As an atheist, faith was not something I'd ever strived for. I had always dealt with problems on my own. They were my problems and I needed to fix them by myself. My parents threw me the keys to life around age eleven and pretty much claimed "You got this!" even though I didn't. But I didn't have a choice—life moves on, whether you've got it or not. I held on and took a bunch of bruises on the way. That was just how life was.

But I had to have faith in Ann and her process. I eventually changed my appointments from nighttime to early Saturday mornings. I wanted to be able to counteract how I was feeling with a chance to at least exercise and go about my day, before coming home at night, feeling like shit and then not being able to sleep.

I had to make changes in my world, because I was changing. My old way of doing things had gotten me here, and keeping up those old ways would have prevented me from making the positive changes I needed to.

After several months of therapy, my wife told me that she and the kids were not walking on eggshells nearly as much. Statements like that felt like a double-edged sword—*I cannot believe what a beast I was to my family*—but I needed to hear them, because my anxiety and PTSD did not want me to recognize that I was finally getting better. According to them, this was all just a waste of time and I should leave therapy immediately and take care of this myself. My mind was—and is still—constantly telling me to address this situation like I used to.

There were times when I would come home after EMDR and just sit on the couch, unable to muster the mental strength to do more. Other days I would spend my day with my family, or in my yard. It took a year or so before I had consistent days of not feeling like I'd been raked over the coals, after sessions.

I was having to unwind what had been done and create a new way of doing things. Old behaviors get you old results, which is why people fail so many times when they need a mental reset, especially when dealing with drugs and alcohol. Self-doubt and low self-esteem can be very harmful to getting better, because they instill doubt that things can improve and change. You fight on two fronts: healing the past, as the present silences all voices of dissent by whatever means necessary.

About a year and a half into therapy, I was struggling mightily. I had plans, after therapy on the upcoming Saturday morning, to go to New York City to meet Garrett and Nick for lunch. I was a mental mess that whole week. I had never before, or since, felt so aware of my emotions in my life. The idea of seeing them again was bringing up very real images of things I had said and done: people, places, everything. It was the most severe mental reckoning I have ever experienced, and I was feeling it physically like I never had before in my life—after having not really felt anxious in fourteen months.

I told my wife about it, which was a new thing for me, and she suggested I exercise. That kept me at bay until Saturday, when I went and saw Ann.

I walked into her office and she could feel the electricity coming off of me. I told her that I was mentally and physically very discombobulated, and exercising had helped me to just barely keep my head above water.

Ann told me I was experiencing an emotional bomb and that she was actually surprised that it had taken me this long, which she attributed to my main defense mechanism, rationalization. We spent that session working on where I was. Having to figure everything out on my own and dealing with consequences, good and bad; as a kid, and up until now, I had just used the rational side of my brain to deal with it. But that only goes so far. I finally was dealing with the emotional side of it, and it had bubbled up and overflowed.

After that session, and a good lunch with friends, I finally passed over the hump and began to consistently feel better. I still have bad days, they're just not as bad as they used to be. It all depends on how I deal with the anxiety and effects of PTSD on a daily basis. I can never forget what happened to me; EMDR doesn't get rid of the memories I have of the trauma I suffered. But it helps me to get through the days better. It has provided me with a process through which I started to heal and restore my mental health.

Saturday, February 29, 2020—Leap Day.

I spent the day writing about going to rehab. It was rough, writing about that period in my life—the only thing worse than living those days is reliving them through writing. It brought up a lot of raw, ugly emotions: guilt, anger, resentment, to name a few. I think of all the things I lost or never had a chance to attain.

A little amped up, I decided to head to the mailbox and see if my fortune would change. I needed a miracle!

I opened up the box and rummaged through the pile, then opened up a nondescript envelope. Lo and behold: the two tickets I'd ordered for the Grateful Dead show, August 1, at Metlife Stadium (Giants Stadium for old Deadheads). Instead of having to trek all the way to Citifield in Queens, we now had a traditional Dead show right here at the stadium, old-school.

I was very excited, commenced my little "Dead ticket acquisition" dance, and hurried inside to spread the bountiful, joyous news. Then I spent the rest of the day typing as best I could. I could probably write a book on the problems of writing this book.

I woke up the next day still pumping with anxiety. I decided to go to the gym and burn off some steam and get myself in a better place. I worked out for about an hour and headed to the car, to spend the rest of the morning writing and then hanging out with my kids.

I got into my car, looked at my phone, and noticed I had a text from my friend DR, another Syracuse native who lives near me. DR's text said that overnight our friend Marc had passed away.

After talking with DR, I went home, told my wife, then went over to Marc's to see his wife. I didn't believe what I had heard until I saw her. I was beyond crushed for his wife and son. Marc was a very stubborn man and had a few health issues, one of which had proved deadly.

When I saw DR the day of the funeral I told him, "We don't know how rich we are until we die," and he nodded in agreement. It was a full funeral home, which is always the wrong time to find out how much you are loved and missed. A human flaw of communication of which we are all guilty.

Marc was buried on March 5; on March 15 the country was locked down due to COVID-19. Now I had another worry on my mind. My father lived alone in Syracuse, independent for a man of his age and health status. Unfortunately, though, he had a couple health issues that made him especially susceptible to the virus: COPD and diabetes. Plus, my dad was about fifty pounds overweight, which certainly did not help with the health challenges we faced as a country.

I was watching the news daily and keeping track of the information being disseminated—the amount of disinformation and incorrect information being provided to the public was disgusting. I was also getting worried about my dad. He grew up with a shitty mom who was also a nurse, and she instilled in him that you listen to your doctor or health experts when it comes to matters of health. My dad also had a famous scientist cousin, George Herbig of the Herbig-Haro Object[11] fame. He had lived through the polio pandemic too—so my dad had been exposed to science, health, and health outbreaks and understood who you should listen to, and why. I was not worried about my dad, though—I was worried about the dummies around him.

I called my dad around March 18 telling him I was worried and asking what he was doing. He didn't sound great, which made me extremely worried. As mentioned, he has the habit of not telling us when he has health issues, a sore subject amongst his children. I told him to be careful and that I was contemplating coming up to get him.

I was watching the news and New York City was falling apart. The northeast was taking the brunt of the virus because even though travel from China was shut down, the United States was still letting people in from Europe. That ban was pretty much useless because people were just changing their reservations and taking connecting flights through Europe. I was beginning to panic; hundreds, if not thousands of people were dying every day. Elmhurst Hospital in Queens, New York was basically a morgue. It was a "war scene of death" and I don't use that term lightly.

I sent my dad a text on March 21 at 7:30 p.m.: "Hey it's getting worse; I am probably coming to get you this week. Call you Sunday morning." I don't think my father got the text. I am not sure he even knows texting is a thing. He's seventy-eight, after all.

I called him the next day and he didn't sound good, but told me he was okay. Another couple hundred people had died, and New Jersey had been shut down for almost a week. I told my wife that I was going to get him and bring him back to our house; she gave her blessing. I called my dad back and told him to be packed and ready to roll Tuesday morning by 7 a.m.

On Tuesday I packed masks, a bunch of snacks, and a few bottles of water. I was not stopping for anything. I was out the door at 4 a.m. and at my dad's apartment at 6 a.m. I have never made such good time—there was absolutely no traffic. There were no state troopers out and I'm not sure they would have stopped me anyway, because they probably didn't have personal protective equipment, since not even the hospitals had enough.

I got to my dad's and he didn't look good. I was sure he didn't have the virus because he would have been dead if he had. I gathered his bags, set the apartment on autopilot, and loaded the car up, him included. I gave him the thrill of his life and stopped by a fast food restaurant for breakfast.

We got to my house and I got my dad inside. He sat down, put NCIS New Orleans on the TV, and his lockdown officially started. Then he casually mentioned that one of the side effects of COPD is the onset of pneumonia, and he thought he had it. He said he was good to let it run its course—he was old and tired, and missed my mom.

I told him I wouldn't let him die on me, though I understood his sadness. His wife of fifty years was gone, his health was deteriorating, and he was coming to peace with an ending. Still, fuck no! You have two grandchildren in this house and you owe them. I was not going to let him walk out on the bill. My house, my rules, motherfucker! Goddamn that felt great, knowing the tables were turned. Except I didn't tell him old people should be seen and not heard.

I called his main doctor, who I knew by name. I gave him the rundown and that he was in New Jersey with me now, then gave my dad the phone, so he could verify his condition and whereabouts. He gave my dad a prescription, which we went and filled right away.

The next thing on the agenda was getting my dad hydrated, and he needed to lose some weight. Okay, a bunch of weight. So, I became the new dietitian of the house. Fruit, oatmeal, and water were new staples. I also went out and got him hydration drinks, which I needed to be careful with because of his diabetes, as their sugar content is dangerous.

In about forty-eight hours my dad had markedly improved. I got salads into his diet and cut down on his overall food consumption. My dad's health improved and he was losing weight. Life was taking on a new normal, despite the madness outside. I was helping my kids with school, because there would not be another outdoor stage built until summer 2021, if we're lucky. My wife was working from home and not going back to the office for the foreseeable future. The world was on fire and I was making sure no one in our house got burned. My family was too damn important to get this virus.

I had already lived through a self-imposed quarantine of sorts with rehab. You could not leave the property, or you were kicked out automatically. I was allowed to leave for AA meetings and work, but had to return immediately. Any deviations, or if you were late outside of a ten-minute grace period, you were expelled. Period!

And because of all these rules, I am here today to write

this book. I was responsible for my own health and well-being and a wrong choice would have put me on a crash course with disaster. My health was important and I needed to keep it as my main focus. People who have gone to rehab or prison were well-equipped to adjust to the pandemic, because we already knew what it was like to be locked down.

At the end of April, my dad started to get a cough and coughed up some very interesting things. He thought the pneumonia was coming back so we called his doctor and decided that we would monitor him closely.

My dad was sleeping in my daughter's room, because he likes unicorns! No, he has bad knees and I didn't want him going up and down any more sets of stairs than needed.

One night I heard a loud thud, flew off the couch, and went to the stairs; my dad was sitting on the top step, looking gray and trying to breathe. I jumped up and grabbed him; he was wearing nylon sport shorts and starting to slide. He slipped down one stair, was leaning against me, and couldn't breathe properly.

I wrapped my arms around him and tried to brace him. All his weight shifted into me and I began to lose my balance. I threw my feet around him and up against the wall to brace myself and keep both of us from tumbling down the stairs. My father was going to die in *my house,* in *my arms.*

My wife was still asleep and I had not brought my phone with me. I called for her, and she got up and looked at us, her eyes wide as saucers. She rushed over to us and asked what was wrong.

"I don't know, he can't get a full breath and I'm taking all his weight." I then replanted my feet because my dad's weight shifted forward down the stairs. My wife ran to get her phone and dialed 911. I kept reassuring my dad he was okay and he was going to live and that I had him. He would have never forgiven me if I was wrong.

My wife put our dog away so he didn't bark at the EMTs, who were there in a matter of minutes. My anxiety was through the roof and I could feel it in my chest. When they arrived, I switched places with one of them. He placed an oxygen mask over my dad's face. After a minute or two, my dad looked better and he wasn't struggling as much. They strapped him up and moved him out. I wasn't allowed to go with him because family was not allowed in the ambulance or hospital, due to COVID-19. I made sure to send my father's cell phone with him so I could find out what was happening.

I stood as they carried him down my front steps to the ambulance, unsure if I ever would see him again.

I talked to my dad the next night; his doctor was kind enough to call. My father was Covid 19–negative, but the pneumonia was back and had hit his lungs very hard. He told me he was going to be there a couple of days and I was forbidden to visit, or even bring in clothes for him because of fear of transmission. He was alive and that was what counted. They put him in his own room and anyone who came in was basically required to wear a hazmat suit.

He also told me that the ambulance had had to wait about twenty minutes before it could get into the dock because the bays were full and other spots were taken up by ambulances that were being disinfected. This was the new normal.

I went and got my dad a few days later, from the children's wing where both of my children were born, at the exit we used when we left the hospital. I got him home and my wife and children were happy to see Pop-Pop. My dad came in and got changed, then came downstairs and went right to my wife and thanked her for all that she did, calling the ambulance and making sure he was alright. My wife reminded my dad of what I did in the process, but he just said, "Yeah, but you gave him permission to do those things." My wife looked at him quizzically, not sure how to respond. She didn't understand that there was a pecking order in my house, growing up. I mowed the lawn and shoveled the snow. Things had not changed, and at least I knew where I still stood.

We are coming to the end of this book. Some of you might ask why I did it. Why write a book about what happened to me? Well, my therapist, Ann, had mentioned to me on numerous occasions that I have a story to tell. That my words could do something that I never ever thought possible: help someone else. She thought I might provide other people with the space to come out and tell their story.

I spurned this idea immediately, the first time I heard it. After about a year and a half more of therapy, Ann mentioned it a few more times, after I had spoken about specific things that had happened in my life, some of which you have read about. It got me thinking about how some famous people who came out and talked about abuses they had suffered had given me enough light, enough room, to feel like maybe my story could be told. Maybe it would help someone else not have to suffer, reminding them that they're not alone.

CHAPTER 18

Breanna Stewart is a professional basketball player for the Seattle Storm of the Women's National Basketball Association. She is a hometown hero of sorts, born in Syracuse, New York. She played ball at a local high school, Cicero-North Syracuse, and went on to have an All-American career at the University of Connecticut and win four national championships.

On October 30, 2017, Ms. Stewart penned an article for the Players' Tribune, a media platform created by ex–New York Yankee Derek Jeter. The title of Ms. Stewart's article was "Me Too" and in it she discussed, in detail, being sexually abused as a child. She says she was inspired after reading McKayla Maroney's account of being sexually abused at Michigan State, by team doctor Larry Nassar, while training for the United States Olympic gymnastics team. Mr. Nassar was accused of sexually abusing up to 250 women since 1992. On January 24, 2018, Mr. Nassar was sentenced to 175 years in prison after admitting to ten charges.

I was stunned to hear of Ms. Stewart's abuse, maybe due to my own naivete to the realities of the world. I already knew of Ms. Maroney, because of the scandal at Michigan State and her famous picture at the London Olympics when she won the silver medal for the vault when she had been projected to win the gold. Now, I could only think that when Ms. Maroney didn't win the gold, she had something else on her mind. I cannot imagine the pressure she was under to win—while being sexually assaulted by one of the adults whose job it was to protect the team.

In Ms. Stewart's article she wrote, "I do know that I'm doing something completely outside of myself by writing this. In fact, this is one of the most difficult things I've ever done and will ever do. But I was recently reading McKayla Maroney's personal account of sexual abuse—one of many powerful stories the #metoo campaign has inspired—and I felt...less alone."[12]

I was stunned to discover that someone knew me, and knew my fear. The last words were the clincher: "less alone." Ms. Stewart, Ms. Maroney, and the women's Olympic gymnastics team that suffered abuse under Larry Nassar are some of the toughest people this country has ever produced.

I knew there were people like me in the world—you read about it in the papers and see it on the news. But after you have been abused, all you feel is alone, and for me, once that aloneness hit, fear, anger, mistrust, anxiety, and other negative emotions swooped in to fill the void. I had been alone since third grade, but maybe these two women, with their stories, could provide me some space, a place where I could speak up and grab some light.

What I never knew until now is, no one ever fights for that space. Without the people who came before, we never would guess that there would be light when we got there. In this instance, I am glad to be wrong.

Jeffrey Wright is an American actor who presently plays Bernard Lowe, head programmer of *Westworld.* He is noted for a diverse range of characters he has played on television, Broadway, and cinema, earning him awards that include Black Reel, Golden Globes, NAACP Image, Emmys, and Tonys. He also, early in his career, portrayed artist Jean-Michel Basquiat in the movie *Basquiat,* which I found to be a great piece of work.

While flipping through the channels one day I came across another piece of his work: a documentary he directed about PTSD, called *We Are Not Done Yet*—in their words, "a creative journey of ten U.S. veterans of varied backgrounds who come together in hopes of battling their traumatic military pasts through the art of written word. Grappling with PTSD, the 'warrior poets' share fears, vulnerabilities, and victories that eventually culminate into a live performance of a collaborative poem.... In the process...these men and women build a new-found tribe in one another, allowing them to share the too often hidden truths about their intimacy with war, death, and trauma."[13]

I don't share the experiences of going to war with these veterans, nor do I think my trauma is the same as theirs. But our trauma does connect us. Trauma is the only thing I know that can take you under and drown you, while everyone around you is walking on water, carrying on with their lives.

The documentary is only forty minutes long, but it took me about a total of four hours to get through the whole thing. My first three times, I had to get up and walk out of my living room, because I could feel the anxiety and PTSD pour through the screen. But that is also the point of the movie: that the average person who does not suffer from, or does not really know about PTSD, can feel the raw emotions it creates, and the destruction it comes with, both mentally and physically. It was Mr. Wright's deep dive into this experiment and the cast's stories that drove me to write this book. If these ladies and gentlemen could get up and tell their story, why not me?

One of the truly hard parts of the movie for me was watching Vainuupo Avegalio, a retired U.S. Army sergeant who sustained multiple injuries while serving overseas. During one part of the movie, he starts to fidget with his hands. To some people that would mean nothing. To me, he was demonstrating with his hands what goes on in my brain. I could feel him, could empathize with what was going through his mind at the time. I could feel his pain because I was in his pain.

After watching each of his castmates talk of their fear, anger, confusion, depression, rejections, and all the other psychological pains they were enduring, I realized I needed to get mine out. And so, in the summer of 2019, I started writing this book. Ann was right: I do have a story to tell.

One of the first places I needed to start was with my friends. I realized that if I was going to write this story that involved them, I would need to tell them my story, or at least the parts they didn't know. My friends are scattered across the U.S., with only a few back in Syracuse. Not knowing when we could all get together, I sat down, created a new document, and wrote down what had happened to me.

I'm ashamed to admit the doubt I experienced, about how they would react. I worried that they wouldn't care, or wouldn't believe me. This is another way for my brain to keep me trapped —despite, time after time, them demonstrating their love for me, I doubted it. It was one of the fiercest clashes my brain would have with itself. It makes you unsure of what you see and know, which is maddening.

I remember when I placed the envelopes in the mailbox. The knot in my throat felt like an iron fist, slowly expanding and trying to cut off my air. I drove away from the post office, swallowing, trying to make it go away, then went home to work on my breathing exercises, trying to get my amygdala to relax.

After a few minutes I felt an unusual sense of calm. I realized what I had done and that the fears that my anxiety was pushing on me were nothing compared to the trust I had of these guys. They had never once let me down. I knew who they were as boys, and now I know who they are as men. I realized I was robbing them of the credit for their character (even if some of them are still Celtics fans).

Waiting for their responses was rough, but my suspicions were right. They reached out with nothing but love and support and I felt such shame for doubting them. The doubt is the worst part, because it makes me doubt my eyes and experiences, even when I feel positively about a situation or person. At times it has made me think I'm crazy.

But now, I realized that their responses were power for me. A power I had never known before, a power most people take for granted.

Thanksgiving 2019 would be my thirtieth high school reunion. I had not given much thought to going because my wife and I hold Thanksgiving at our house with my sister, her husband, my wife's mom, and my dad.

Once I found out the guys were going, though, I was up for it. It would be nice to see everyone in one place again, instead of our large group texts.

As I was driving to the bar for the reunion, my mind was going through all the normal questions: who is going, how will they look, do they like the Grateful Dead?

I walked into the bar and one of the Birds was sitting right at the front door. I gave my hellos and moved on, said hello to some classmates, and milled about.

When I ran into a second of the Three Birds, it slowly dawned upon me: *This is the first time I have ever been in public with these people that I'm not living in fear of my secret.* The Birds didn't know of my secret, just my guy friends, but I still had this great sense of freedom. I had never felt that way before. I was making progress with my book and had already made the decision to self-publish, so eventually they will find out. But my friends' support and outreach after my letter had already made all the difference.

A grin came over my face. I was free and no one could take that away from me. I was finally different, in a good way. I have never felt anything like that before, and it was beautiful.

The night went on and my secret was still intact, but the world had completely changed. *I am going to get on that stage and there will be some light for me.* And you never have to push anyone out of the way, there is always room.[HC1]

I know that coming out and telling someone about being abused, or raped, or that you're struggling with mental illness seems hard. I will not sugarcoat it and tell you it will be easy. Some people may not believe you; some may even accuse you of having an agenda, or wanting to hurt someone. Unfortunately, society has proven it will disregard and even ignore people like me. In the news we have seen entertainers, politicians, white-collar professionals, and even everyday citizens walk free after their sexual harassment, abuse, or rape becomes known.

But you cannot let that determine whether you want to

speak up. I say fuck that—speak up and speak out. Don't listen to what anyone says, but pay close attention to what they do, who they do it with, and why. Actions always speak louder than words.

You won't be judged by the words you say, but by the people you surround yourself with and the actions that you take. Words are meaningless if they are not backed up by action. I have lived by this since the day I was abused—I had to. I heard too many voices in this world preaching one thing, and then doing another. That is dangerous for someone like me. I cannot have people near me or my family whose actions don't match their rhetoric. I would be putting us in danger.

If you talk to my friends, or anyone that knew me in middle school or high school, they'll tell you I never wanted my life to turn out this way. I never had the intention of becoming an alcoholic, nor did I wish I could fuck up my life and completely screw myself out of twelve years of living. Whether in rehab, the halfway house, or an Alcoholics Anonymous meeting, I never heard anyone say that this was what they had planned, that they were glad they ruined their lives, relationships with lovers, friends, marriages, family members—all shot to shit because that was their intention.

I spent a lot of time with my friends, either in school, playing sports, or hanging out on weekend nights. Running around with guys I loved gave me space to survive. After high school graduation—when I lost my friends and that exercise—the slow unraveling of my life began.

I don't know about other people with anxiety, so I will only speak for myself. Alcohol acts to combat anxiety by relaxing me. It's like a trick birthday candle.

Say we go out after work on Friday to catch a drink after a long week. We both sit down and order a beer. For me, the beer will initially take the edge off, but then like a trick birthday candle, *poof,* the anxiety pops right back up. My brain then tells me that I have not successfully suppressed the anxiety and I should have another drink.

Alcoholism does not happen overnight, but over time—and you don't think of these actions in the long term until you can't get out from under it. In rehab, I saw all sorts of people with all different stories about how they ended up there; they were filled with pain, loss, fear, anger, disappointment, destruction. Marriages that were lost, jobs that were lost…stories that invited the teller to crack open a bottle of wine and forget.

I thought, when Bruce committed suicide, that my problems were over. I knew he was dead and he could never hurt me or anyone ever again. What I didn't know was that the trauma he caused would boil in me. Keeping my secret didn't turn it in to a beautiful aged Italian red wine; instead, it turned to boiling-hot vinegar.

The "if-then" statements that ran through my mind the night of the abuse turned into a mental pattern that I still suffer from to this day. Everyone I meet and everything I do must be run through this process, whether I like it or not. If my mind deems you unsafe, I cannot be around you. And once you make the list, you are on it forever.

I have disassociated from people as I have come to know them because they are dangerous. Narcissists are the worst and most dangerous. The problem is they are phony up front and it takes time to find out who they are. They are completely untrustworthy. I dated one once and I am glad she dumped me because that could have gotten dangerous. Narcissists are like mental terrorists.

I have to warn anyone who wishes to make their abuse known: for the most part, society doesn't care about us. Two of the most dangerous words for a person who has been abused to hear are "yeah, but." When you watch TV, the news, interviews, talk shows, you will see people of different colors, religions, socioeconomic status, and you can witness them making an excuse for bad sexual behavior with a "yeah, but" statement. They breeze through the words and there is very rarely pushback.

I don't want you to be discouraged, or put off by those "yeah, but" statements. First, let it be motivation to make those people uncomfortable. Let our message be something that they cannot shake or roll over. Second, the deniers tell abused people the most important thing they can about a person: their price. They tell you what they are willing to overlook to get what they want or need. "Yeah, but" lets people know that they are willing to overlook the pain, fear, anger, and misery of someone who was abused, so they can make a profit. It also lets you know a lot about their character. Never trust words not backed up by deeds in the "yeah, but" crowd.

I hope there are people who read my story and feel inspired to share theirs. I hope there are people who seek help from licensed professionals to assist them in their travels of healing their pain and anguish over what has happened to them.

There are days you may not want to get out of bed and deal with what has been dealt to you. But trust me when I say there are better days ahead. As an atheist, the only reason I know there is a better tomorrow is because I have had so many horrible yesterdays. I hoped at times there would be no tomorrow, only to wake up and be proven wrong, time and again. But getting through those tomorrows got me to today. And today is better.

I am angry sometimes that I got abused, and you would be too. It is not an anger I can just turn off; if that was the case, no one would ever suffer from trauma. I wish I could. I can never forget what happened to me. I can only gain tools to help me deal with it and carry on.

One more very important note here, and I want everyone to remember this: a person who wears a uniform does not deserve any more respect than someone who doesn't. My brother Bruce, who was given his uniform by the United States Marine Corps, is a perfect example. When we went out to eat with my grandmother in Massachusetts and that man was explaining to his wife who Bruce was, I wanted to rush over and say, "He's a drug dealer, a sexual abuser, he committed assaults, including one on a cop. He also kept his family imprisoned in a total hell—

but yeah, that uniform is way fucking snazzy."

If you wear a uniform, or hold a public position, you have to earn our respect. Adulation of a uniform, or position, without holding accountable who is in it, just empowers a shitbag to be a shitbag. Give people the respect all humans deserve, but wait and see if they can meet your expectations before idolizing them. The permissions we as a society give to those who abuse others needs to stop.

Every person's life is a song and our actions are the lyrics. Don't let the song end before its time! Once you leave the garden of your youth, you cannot make it grow again. You must remember the flowers you saw.

Epilogue
by Cori Herbig

When Pete asked me to write something for his book, my first reaction was apprehension. I was worried that he wouldn't like what I had to say, and I knew I couldn't lie about how hard it's been. His response took me aback. "Do you honestly think you can hurt me any more than I've hurt you? I terrorized you and the kids."

I was shocked. Not only by his words, but also by his ability to be introspective and contrite about his past actions. He was not always able to admit past mistakes in such an honest and open way, without spiraling into self-deprecation. So I agreed, and here I am.

To be clear, "terrorize" is not the word I would have chosen to describe his actions. There was never any physical abuse. If there had been, I would have taken our two children and left. There was, undoubtedly, verbal intimidation and a lot of gaslighting. And tension—so much tension. I used to refer to our home as a powder keg.

It became a vicious cycle. He would yell about something that to me felt like nothing big—more than yell, he would explode, leaving the kids reduced to tears, and me trying to shield them from his rage. He would stomp out and I would whisper to the kids that it was okay, and that "Daddy is just having a bad morning." Pete would interpret the whispering as me undermining him and siding with the kids, which would fuel his anger even more.

I found myself increasingly at a loss as to how to navigate these situations, which were happening more and more often. And I found myself worrying more and more that it was doing irreparable harm to our children. This pattern played out for years.

Having kids is hard for even the most mentally stable people, but for someone with Pete's history of trauma and anxiety, it pushed him over the edge, to a point where he struggled to control his anger. When I found myself coaching our two young children about how to walk on eggshells around their father so they wouldn't set him off, I knew something had to change.

When we met, Pete seemed so excited about life and everything he had ahead of him. It was almost electric. There was no way that I could've known then that what I thought was excitement and *joie de vivre* was actually a hidden manifestation of deep-seated anxiety from a childhood filled with trauma and uncertainty. It wasn't until Pete and I both better understood the impact that his childhood had had on his emotional and mental well-being that we would truly be able to begin to heal and develop the healthy relationship and family life that I had hoped for when we first met.

Before we had kids, I was able to mostly brush off any reactions from Pete that felt disproportionately outsized to me. I was able to put my feelings in a box and disengage from him until he calmed down. Once the kids entered the scene, it wasn't so easy. One night in particular, probably around December of 2013, I found myself standing in our three-year-old son's room, holding our infant daughter, physically blocking our son from Pete because I was scared he was going to hit him. I will never know if he actually would've hit him if I hadn't intervened. I tried to kick Pete out of our home that night. He refused to go, but it sparked a series of events that led us to where we are now, and for that I am grateful.

I gave Pete an ultimatum. We could speak to a counselor or he could leave. The choice was his. We tried a few different therapists back then, none of whom really seemed able to connect with Pete. But the experience itself seemed to take the edge off just enough for us to continue to exist without our family imploding.

It was also around this time that Pete began smoking marijuana multiple times a day. On some level, I knew that he was self-medicating, but emotionally, I felt like he was avoiding his problems by being high all the time, in addition to spending money that we really didn't have to spare. Pete's work history has been spotty at best since I have known him. After he lost his job when I was six months pregnant with our daughter, money got tight, and I began to suspect that Pete wasn't cut out for a typical 9-5 office job. I had often said that it sometimes felt as if Pete spoke a different language than I do, and I suspected that this was playing out in the workplace as well, making it difficult for Pete to find a place he belonged professionally.

Not every incident rose to the level of the one in December of 2013. In fact, most were easier to just swallow and move on. There were times when Pete's anxiety was so palpable that I knew it was coming before he did. I don't think either of us had any idea how bad it would get once our second child was born.

On the day we left the hospital with her, I remember Pete walking about ten feet ahead of me down the hospital corridors. He was carrying the baby in the infant car seat, and I, about thirty hours post-partum, was trying to keep up. It felt to me like he was seething, burdened, and trying to escape. What should have been an incredibly joyous time for our family was overshadowed by Pete's inability to allow the joy to overtake his anxiety.

While Pete has always been exceedingly protective of me and the kids with respect to any outside threat, he sometimes could not see how his own actions were harming us. I felt alone that day. I questioned whether we should have had a second child at all, which left me wracked with guilt. I questioned whether I should have tied my life to his. And I questioned whether I should stay.

This was not the only time I struggled with these feelings. It took hardcore suppression for me to push down what, at times, felt like a clear knowing that we were destined for a reckoning that would inevitably lead to the demise of our marriage – until we finally found a therapist who helped us, and who mentioned the possibility that Pete might have post-traumatic stress disorder.

Being married to someone with PTSD messes not only with your partner's head, but with yours too. Because I couldn't understand what was going on inside Pete, and he wasn't in a place to be able to talk to me about it openly, I was left to try to figure it out, and the pieces didn't fit. I couldn't understand why Pete would escalate the way he did, or how to help him through his own struggles.

One of the hardest days in our marriage for me was the day that Pete told me (in a therapy session) that I couldn't help him. Helping people is in my DNA. It's what I do. And it broke my heart to hear him say that.

If we hadn't entered couples counseling, which led to Pete starting EMDR, I am 100 percent certain that our marriage would be over by now. Frankly, one of the most powerful things that kept me in our marriage in those early days was the kids. I don't mean "We stayed together for the kids" in the cliché sense. What I mean is that the thought of him parenting without me there to shield the kids from his rage was unimaginable to me. Not being able to protect my kids, particularly when they cried, which was a clear trigger for Pete, was something I could not risk back in those days. I didn't trust him to control his anger, and he knew it. This only complicated things and inflamed the tension between us.

Over the years, and with a lot of hard work, Pete has gotten dramatically better about recognizing when he's being triggered and stepping away or doing deep breathing to calm down before he interacts with our daughter when she's crying. But even now, I sometimes have a lingering anxiety that I won't be there and he'll scream at her when she's crying. At one point, I even taught her that when she needed to cry, "Daddy is not the person you go to. Come to me." She immediately questioned me about what to do if I wasn't there, and I placed the outsized burden of emotionally supporting her on her older brother, who was still a child himself. It didn't occur to me at the time that I was perpetuating a fear that needed to be unraveled, not built upon.

It's a process for all of us to not only do the changing ourselves, but to allow each other to change as well. Pete probably
hasn't yelled at our daughter for crying in well over a year, but I
still tense up with anticipation when she cries, waiting for him
to explode. I am learning alongside Pete and trying my hardest
not to expect reactions from him that were common in the past,
but haven't happened in a long, long time. It's unfair of me to expect those same old reactions from him, but sometimes change
is hard, especially when you're so close to the situation.

I know I'm not the only one in our family who experiences this kind of secondary trauma. Our kids know that "When
Daddy is in a bad mood, just let him be." At very young ages,
they learned how to recognize it when their father was "having
a rough morning," and they know to steer clear of him. They
know when he is already tense and he asks them to do something, not to delay or talk back. Our son has mastered this better
than our daughter, who is still too young to always be able to
control her impulse to argue with him. I write all of this while
also re-reading the paragraph just above this one. These types
of interactions are now few and far between in our home, but
there's part of me that still anticipates and expects them none-
theless, demonstrating just how far the trauma created by one
person can reach.

I am grateful that our kids don't really remember when
things were truly volatile in our home. They were too little. The
difference between then and now is truly staggering. Our home
was at a nine out of ten on the volatility scale back then, and
these days it's probably at about a two, some days even lower. But
I also have no doubt that they will have some underlying trauma
from it that they will have to unpack later in life.

I know that Pete loves me and the kids. The kids know it
too, and they adore him. I know that he would do anything for
us. And I know that he has been working incredibly hard over
the last five years to deal with his past, in order to set our present
and future on a path that keeps our family intact and healthy.

Reading his book has given me so much insight into why

Pete is who he is, and why he sometimes reacts the way he does. Things that never made any sense to me are suddenly clear. Before reading his book, I never understood why Christmas was always so hard for him. It was like no matter what I did to make the day fun for our family, he just couldn't enjoy it (or let us enjoy it). After learning about the inextricable ties to Bruce Jr. that Christmas holds for Pete, it makes so much more sense.

After reading about the many nights that Pete lay awake in his bed, fearing for his safety as a young child, his chronic insomnia makes so much more sense.

After learning about how keeping his secret for decades hardwired Pete to believe that there was no one he could trust, I better understand why he has withheld his feelings from me so often. I can't even count the number of times we've argued over the years when he has said "You see! This is why I don't tell you how I feel," which always baffled me. In my pre-Pete experience, when two people argue, both say how they feel and work toward understanding and resolution. With Pete, for years, us disagreeing inevitably led to him shutting down, withdrawing, or spiraling into a rage. It left so much unresolved, and added even further to the tension in our home.

This book has also allowed me to see some interesting parallels between Pete and his dad, like how Pete's sister was able to bring their dad out of his emotional shell in ways that no one else had. I watch our daughter do that with Pete every day. I watch him laugh and joke and interact with her in ways that he doesn't with anyone else. And I watch her push his buttons like no one else can without sending him spiraling. I watched Pete hold his breath until our son passed seven years of age, knowing that that was the age at which his own life was forever altered in ways he wouldn't understand until decades later. I watched him breathe a sigh of relief when he realized that our son was safe from the kind of trauma that he himself had endured at that young age.

EMDR is not a magic bullet. There has been so much progress, but there have also been setbacks—like the morning in 2018 when Pete physically blocked my exit from the bathroom in the middle of a heated fight, and I found myself scared for my physical safety. He never crossed the line though. He calmed down, and we talked about it, and he spent an inordinate amount of time unpacking that event with his therapist, Ann.

Or like the time we were at my grandmother's funeral and Pete spiraled into a rage about something, leaving me feeling unsupported and resentful that my husband couldn't figure out how to be there for me in my time of need.

There are countless examples of how Pete's anxiety and PTSD have made my life nearly impossible at times. I have had to reach deep and find strength I didn't know I had, but so has Pete. I went to see Ann with him once, at her request. She told me that statistically, Pete was an anomaly. Apparently, only one in about 100,000 people who endure the kind of abuse and trauma that Pete has don't either commit suicide or end up addicted to opioids. She told me that the work he was doing there each week was tantamount to swimming through a river of vomit, filled with razor blades.

I know that Pete took on this seemingly insurmountable task for me and the kids. I also know that by now, he's doing it as much for himself as he is for us. Either way, I am more grateful than words can say for his willingness to do the hard work to save himself and our family. To say that I am proud of Pete for all that he has worked so hard to overcome is a massive understatement. What he has done, and continues to do, is nothing short of extraordinary.

After nearly five years of EMDR with Ann, I finally feel like Pete and I speak the same language. I am forever indebted to Ann for helping him come to terms with his past, which has allowed him to more fully embrace his present and future.

And whether this book sells one copy (to me) or one million copies, I am in awe of his perseverance and his ability to connect the pieces of his past to form a new, better future for me, our children, and himself.

Oh I get the last word.

For the last forty years I have been watching society deal with abusers and the abused. I have seen the same bullshit sentences handed down to abusers and the abused get run over time after time. As a whole, society does not care about me anymore than they care about our female Olympic gymnastic team. Oh yes, there is initial outrage, but it always fades, even when more and more disturbing details are divulged. Watching society react to people like me makes me believe more and more the safest thing for me at the time was to keep my mouth shut. Forty years of watching society disregard [HC2]females who have been abused makes me think I would have never been believed. We still do not believe the woman lying on a gurney, faced bruised, clothes torn, and a detailed account of the event. She still gets asked about her previous sexual experiences, what she was wearing, why she was alone. Does that sound like people who would support me?

I have been running through my life since the abuse with anchors tied to my back – various sizes and lengths of rope, but anchors that cause great amounts of damage. Sometimes those anchors catch, and I would ruin whatever I came in contact with. Other times the anchors nicked, and crashed into things in my life and I did not care, could not see the destruction. It was not until now that I am able to start cutting the ropes.

When I sat down to write this book I had no idea where it would go. I put a stream of three-hundred and thirty thousand unconscious words on paper. Some days I could write up to ten pages, others, just two. Statistically, I should not be here and when I look back on my life, I wonder how I am. I was put in a prison cell, and although I could come and go through the door as I wish, it is still a cell. Those walls are with me forever and the time I spent in therapy just gave me ways to make that cell more comfortable.

People always worry about abusers. It is funny how you can listen to details of some twenty-something year old shitbag rape a girl and you will have people demand that we think of the abuser and how his life may be ruined – how the abuser is going to have a hard time building their life after jail, or how their reputation would be tarnished. Really? The last thing we should ever be worried about as a society is the abuser. Instead, it is the "go to." The worries of the abuser should never be considered and anyone supporting them should be called out.

I do not know if this book will ever be read. I do not know if anyone would give their money to read my words. I'm a no one. Someone who has never done a thing in life. My only hope is that if one person could read this and not end up like me, I win. I want people to know that you do not have to be dragged down the same set of razorblades in life that I was. There is no need to put yourself through a grinder like I did. Stand up and shout, and make the bitches fear you!

The picture on the last page is me and my siblings, dated Spring 1972. That is my sister holding me about to earth slam. My brother Bruce is the one on the right. Look at his eyes. Those do not look like the eyes of what should be a happy boy's life. They look like pain and fear. Shakespeare said, "eyes are windows into the soul." Those eyes tell me something was wrong and it was never fixed. I imagine that those are the eyes he was looking through when he killed himself. I have finally removed my own sunglasses on life.

Acknowledgments

My thanks and love to my wife and kids, support from my sister, my brother, my parents, Garrett, Dan, Larry, Jamie, Steve, Dave, Peter, Jamie, Bob, and Chris, my cousin C for playing ball, the Three Birds (thanks for the cigarette light), LG, the graduating class of 1989 Bulldogs, the Grateful Dead, Phish, Poppy's arm, my therapist Ann, lacrosse, the love and support I have received over the years from people, the Ronco smokeless ashtray, GLH-9 hair in a spray can, and Ronco Mr. Microphone ("Hey good lookin', we'll be back to pick you up later"), which I think made one of my dogs sterile.

To the National Collegiate Athletic Association (NCAA) rumor has it you are interested in securing a lacrosse trophy. No worries, we believe it is buried in a safe location. Oh, and just suck it. Really, just suck it!

To NASA- screw you for canceling Dr. Jeanette Epps space flight!

RESOURCES[14]

If you are experiencing an emergency, please call 911.

Domestic Violence and Intimate Partner Violence

National Domestic Violence Hotline

1 (800) 799-7233

Available 24 hours a day, 7 days a week via phone and online chat.

The hotline is available for anyone experiencing domestic violence, seeking resources or information, or questioning unhealthy aspects of their relationship.

Love Is Respect – National Teen Dating Abuse Hotline

Hotline: 1 (866) 331-9474
Text: 22522

Available 24 hours a day, 7 days a week via phone, text, and online chat.

Love Is Respect offers information, support, and advocacy to young people who have questions or concerns about their dating relationships.

StrongHearts Native Helpline

1 (844) 762-8483

Available Monday through Friday, 9 a.m. to 5:30 p.m. CST via phone.

The StrongHearts Native Helpline is a safe, anonymous, and confidential service for Native Americans experiencing domestic violence and dating violence.

Pathways to Safety International

Hotline: 1 (833) 723 – 3833
Email: crisis@pathwaystosafety.org
Available 24 hours a day, 7 days a week via phone, email, and online chat.

Pathways to Safety International assists Americans experiencing interpersonal and gender-based violence abroad.

Women's Law

Email hotline: https://hotline.womenslaw.org/

The WomensLaw online helpline provides basic legal information, referrals, and emotional support for victims of abuse.

LGBTQIA+

Gay, Lesbian, Bisexual and Transgender National Hotline

Hotline: 1 (888) 843-4564

Youth Talkline: 1 (800) 246-7743

Senior Helpline: 1 (888) 234-7243

Email: help@LGBThotline.org

Hours vary, available via phone and online chat.

The LGBT National Help Center serves gay, lesbian, bisexual, transgender, and questioning people by providing free and confidential peer support and local resources.

Sexual Assault

Rape, Abuse, and Incest National Network (RAINN) – National Sexual Assault Hotline

1 (800) 656-4673

Available 24 hours a day, 7 days a week via phone and online chat.

RAINN (Rape, Abuse and Incest National Network) is the nation's largest anti–sexual violence organization. RAINN created and operates the National Sexual Assault Hotline (800.656.HOPE, online.rainn.org y rainn.org/es) in partnership with more than 1,000 local sexual assault service providers across the country. RAINN also operates the DoD Safe Helpline for the Department of Defense. RAINN carries out programs to prevent sexual violence, help survivors, and ensure that perpetrators are brought to justice.

Department of Defense (DOD) Safe Helpline for Sexual Assault

1 (877) 995-5247

Available 24 hours a day, 7 days a week via phone and online chat.

The DOD Safe Helpline is a crisis support service designed to provide sexual assault services for survivors, their loved ones, and other members of the DOD community.

Human Trafficking

National Human Trafficking Hotline

Hotline: 1 (888) 373-7888

Text: 233733

The National Human Trafficking Hotline is a national anti-trafficking hotline serving victims and survivors of human trafficking and the anti-trafficking community in the United States. The toll-free hotline is available to answer calls from anywhere in the country, 24 hours a day, 7 days a week, every day of the year in more than 200 languages.

Youth

National Runaway Safeline

Hotline: 1 (800) 786-2929

Email: info@1800runaway.org

Available 24 hours a day, 7 days a week via phone, email, forum, and online chat.

The National Runaway Safeline provides crisis and support services for homeless and runaway youth in the United States.

National Center for Missing and Exploited Children (NCMEC)

Hotline: 1 (800) 843-5678

Cyber Tipline: http://www.missingkids.com/gethelpnow/cybertipline

NCMEC serves as a clearinghouse and comprehensive reporting center for all issues related to the prevention of and recovery from child victimization.

ChildHelp National Child Abuse Hotline

Hotline: 1 (800) 422-4453
Available 24 hours a day, 7 days a week via phone and text.

The ChildHelp National Child Abuse Hotline is dedicated to the prevention of child abuse. Serving the U.S. and Canada, the hotline is staffed 24 hours a day, 7 days a week with professional crisis counselors who—through interpreters—provide assistance in over 170 languages. The hotline offers crisis intervention, information, and referrals to thousands of emergency, social service, and support resources. All calls are confidential.

Boystown USA – Your Life Your Voice Helpline

Hotline: 1 (800) 448-3000
Text: Text VOICE to 20121 (hours vary)
Available 24 hours a day, 7 days a week via phone, email, text, and online chat.

Your Life Your Voice is a program of Boystown USA and is available to children, parents, and families who are struggling with self-harm, mental health disorders, and abuse.

Mental Health and Substance Abuse

National Suicide Prevention Lifeline

Hotline: 1 (800) 273-8255
Available 24 hours a day, 7 days a week via phone and online chat.

The National Suicide Prevention Lifeline provides free and confidential support for people in distress, prevention and crisis resources for you or your loved ones, and best practices for professionals.

National Alliance on Mental Illness (NAMI) Helpline

Hotline: 1 (800) 950-6264
Email: info@nami.org
Available Monday through Friday, 10 a.m. to 6 p.m. Eastern Standard Time.

The NAMI Helpline assists individuals and families who have questions about mental health disorders, treatment, and support services.

Substance Abuse and Mental Health Services Administration

(SAMHSA) Helpline
Hotline: 1 (800) 662-4357
Available 24 hours a day, 7 days a week via phone in English and Spanish.

SAMHSA's National Helpline provides free and confidential treatment referral and information services for individuals and families facing mental and/or substance abuse disorders.

Contact the Victim Connect Hotline by phone at 1-855-4-VIC-TIM or by chat for more information or assistance in locating services that can help you or a loved one.

Once in a while, you get shown the light
In the strangest of places if you look at it right[15]

Later bitches-
Pete

---

[1]"Breathe," (2 AM) lyrics by Anna Nalick

[2]"Porch Song," lyrics: David A. Schools, Domingo Ortiz, John F. Bell, John R. Herman, Michael N. Houser, S. Ortiz, Todd A. Nance Song: Widespread Panic

[3]"El Cóndor Pasa (If I Could)," music by Daniel Alomia Robles, lyrics by Paul Simon, performed by Simon and Garfunkel

[4]"The Gold It's In The..." by Pink Floyd, lyrics by Roger Waters and David Gilmour

[5] Song by Bo Diddley-Lyrics by Ellas McDaniel

[6]*The Root* by Eric Hammel, page 295

[7]*The Root* by Eric Hammel, page 303

[8]"Dreams," lyrics by Gregg Allman, Song- The Allman Brothers Band.

[9]"The Other One" by the Grateful Dead, lyrics and music by Bob Weir and Bill Kreutzman

[10]"Wharf Rat" by the Grateful Dead, lyrics by Robert Hunter and Jerry Garcia

[11]   https://hubblesite.org/contents/media/images/1999/35/902-Image.html

[12]https://www.theplayerstribune.com/en-us/articles/breanna-stewart-me-too

[13]http://wearenotdoneyetfilm.com/

[14] Victim Connect https://victimconnect.org/resources/national-hotlines/

[15] Scarlet Begonias- Words by Robert Hunter Music by Jerry Garcia

Made in the USA
Columbia, SC
14 January 2022

54269323R00150